Presented to:

●————————————————————————————————●

From:

●————————————————————————————————●

Date:

●————————————————————————————————●

Endorsements

When I work with clients who are in a season of waiting or even when I struggle with waiting in my own life, there is a feeling of being stuck or trapped, accompanied by a sense of hopelessness or resignation. What Barb has captured in *Seasons of Waiting* is the expectancy and the discipline of approaching waiting as a way of pursuing balance between the active pursuit of God's presence, and the rest found in the assurance of His promises. Barb integrates her work as a counselor with solid biblical examples and practical exercises that will shift your mindset on the experience of waiting to one of purpose and partnership with God and with others. If you've struggled in a season of waiting or find yourself in one right now, this book will compel you to reconsider the story of waiting that God is writing in your soul, and to embrace a new narrative that includes opportunities for curiosity, hope, and courage.

DR. DEBORAH GORTON
Clinical psychologist, professor, author of *Embracing Uncomfortable: Facing Our Fears While Pursuing Our Purpose*

Seasons of Waiting is unique as it merges the world of faith and mental health with so much grace and wisdom. Barb's insight as a counselor shines a beautiful light on not giving up hope while we navigate the not-so-easy seasons of waiting for our dreams and promises to be fulfilled, and as we learn to trust God with the process of our growth. This book will come as such an encouragement to those who find themselves on a journey of longing and waiting.

ADRIENNE CAMP
Author and musician

Barb Hill is a talented writer and gifted storyteller. She doesn't just give us an invitation to hope, she gives us the permission we desperately need to wrestle with the paradox of hope and pain in seasons of waiting. Whether we're waiting for someone to love, something steady to hold onto, a change in our circumstances, or a shift in our perspective, Barb reminds us that seasons of waiting also hold the potential and possibility to bring out the best in us if we're willing to wait with hope.

BETH GRAYBILL
Consultant, teacher, and storyteller

Seasons of Waiting not only offers encouraging revelations to those who find themselves journeying through the process of waiting, but author Barb Hill offers keen insights on how to walk that road with thoughtful and joyful hope. Her beautiful, personal approach to writing, colored by the wisdom she has gleaned from her years as a therapist, make this book an excellent read for those in a season of waiting, or those who simply wish to consider how they might respond to the God-ordained purpose of each moment.

GINNY OWENS
Singer/songwriter, author, teacher, and advocate

Seasons of Waiting

52 DEVOTIONS

SEASONS

OF *Waiting*

An Invitation To Hope

Written by **Barb Hill**, LPC-MHSP
Illustrated by **Shealeen Louise Bishop**

Tyndale House Publishers
Carol Stream, Illinois

LIVING
EXPRESSIONS
COLLECTION

Visit Tyndale online at tyndale.com.

Visit the author at barbhillauthor.com.

Visit the illustrator at shealeenlouise.com.

Tyndale, Tyndale's quill logo, *Living Expressions*, and the Living Expressions logo are registered trademarks of Tyndale House Ministries.

Seasons of Waiting: An Invitation to Hope

Copyright © 2022 by Barbara M. Hill. All rights reserved.

Cover and all interior illustrations copyright © Shealeen Louise Bishop. All rights reserved.

Author photograph copyright © 2022 by KT Sura. All rights reserved.

Illustrator's photograph copyright © 2022 by Shealeen Louise Bishop. All rights reserved.

Designed by Sarah Susan Richardson

Edited by Erin Keeley Marshall

The story poem featured on page *xix* is excerpted from *Morning Dew Drops: Bloom Where You Are Planted* by Norma Boone, published by WestBow Press in 2020. Used by permission.

Unless otherwise indicated, all Scripture quotations are taken from The Passion Translation,® copyright © 2017, 2018 by Passion & Fire Ministries, Inc. Used by permission. All rights reserved. ThePassionTranslation.com.

Scripture quotations marked AMP are taken from the Amplified® Bible (AMP), copyright © 2015 by The Lockman Foundation. Used by permission. www.lockman.org.

Scripture quotations marked AMPC are taken from the Amplified® Bible (AMPC), copyright © 1954, 1958, 1962, 1964, 1965, 1987 by The Lockman Foundation. Used by permission. www.lockman.org.

Scripture quotation marked CEV is taken from the Contemporary English Version, copyright © 1991, 1992, 1995 by American Bible Society. Used by permission.

Scripture quotation marked DLNT is taken from the *Disciples' Literal New Testament*, copyright © 2011 by Michael J. Magill. Used by permission. All rights reserved.

Scripture quotations marked ESV are from The ESV® Bible (The Holy Bible, English Standard Version®), copyright © 2001 by Crossway, a publishing ministry of Good News Publishers. Used by permission. All rights reserved.

Scripture quotations marked MSG are taken from *The Message*, copyright © 1993, 2002, 2018 by Eugene H. Peterson. Used by permission of NavPress. All rights reserved. Represented by Tyndale House Publishers.

Scripture quotations marked NASB are taken from the (NASB®) New American Standard Bible,® copyright © 1960, 1971, 1977, 1995, 2020 by The Lockman Foundation. Used by permission. All rights reserved. www.lockman.org.

Scripture quotation marked NCV is taken from the New Century Version.® Copyright © 2005 by Thomas Nelson, Inc. Used by permission. All rights reserved.

Scripture quotations marked NIV are taken from the Holy Bible, *New International Version,® NIV*.® Copyright © 1973, 1978, 1984, 2011 by Biblica, Inc.® Used by permission. All rights reserved worldwide.

Scripture quotations marked NKJV are taken from the New King James Version,® copyright © 1982 by Thomas Nelson. Used by permission. All rights reserved.

Scripture quotations marked NLT are taken from the *Holy Bible*, New Living Translation, copyright © 1996, 2004, 2015 by Tyndale House Foundation. Used by permission of Tyndale House Publishers, Carol Stream, Illinois 60188. All rights reserved.

Scripture quotation marked TLB is taken from *The Living Bible*, copyright © 1971 by Tyndale House Foundation. Used by permission of Tyndale House Publishers, Carol Stream, Illinois 60188. All rights reserved.

Scripture quotation marked VOICE is taken from The Voice.™ Copyright © 2012 by Ecclesia Bible Society. Used by permission. All rights reserved.

For information about special discounts for bulk purchases, please contact Tyndale House Publishers at csresponse@tyndale.com, or call 1-855-277-9400.

ISBN 978-1-4964-6223-7

Printed in China

28	27	26	25	24	23	22
7	6	5	4	3	2	1

To my late grandmother,

Mary Lou Sasso.

Even though you are not physically here,

your spirit remains, and is felt every day

in the deep faith and hope you always held for me.

Contents

Foreword

I first met Barb in Southern California when she was an intern at an organization I worked for. At the time, I had no idea how much life we would eventually share. We went on to organize events and travel (and experience almost-missed flights) together. The two of us spent many evenings laughing, crying, and eating Mexican food—usually all at the same time. After nearly eight years of friendship and countless texts and phone calls, there's one topic, one supremely human struggle, that we often come back to: the process of waiting.

None of us enjoy waiting—not for a plate of tacos, not for a promotion, not for a spouse. We prefer our desires to be delivered on our terms and time line. But none of us can avoid waiting, can we? It greets us around every corner through painful delays and the ache of deferred hope. In these moments, we face tough choices to release control and courageously wait with hope. Even more than that, our waiting seasons present us with opportunities to be transformed.

Seasons of Waiting is not only an invitation to hope but also to be transformed. To come as you are, but to leave changed. To let go of what doesn't belong and embrace what does. To wrestle with the doubts and questions and experience God's presence and overwhelming peace. To be more convinced than ever that God cares as much about the state of our hearts as he does about our heart's desires.

Barb isn't on the sidelines shouting empty clichés about waiting and hope; she's in the game with you, sharing from the depth of her heart and lived experience.

In each devotion you're about to read, Barb shows up as a compassionate therapist, a kindred friend, and an honest human to offer a fresh perspective about what it means to wait with intention and a heart full of hope. She gently corrects the false narratives that say waiting is a passive experience where you cross your fingers and simply hope something changes. She offers a better and more true narrative—that waiting is empowered participation with God to bring transformation and a deeper experience of wholeness for body, mind, and spirit.

Bianca Juárez Olthoff
Pastor, podcaster, and bestselling author of How to Have Your Life Not Suck

Author's Note

This book has been in my heart for a long time, and it brings me so much joy that you are holding it in your hands. Naval Ravikant says, "To write a great book, you must first become the book."[1] The process of becoming this book began well before I was gifted the opportunity to write it and continues to be one of my most challenging experiences.

Although I have navigated many seasons of waiting, the one that has remained in my life until now is waiting for a family of my own. Through each season, I have needed to learn how to navigate this particularly painful experience of waiting.

Yet this is not a book only about waiting for a family. I wanted to be very intentional about how I share my story so you can find your own within these pages, even if our waiting experiences look different. My hope is that every part of you feels honored—mind, body, and spirit—as you move through this book. I endeavor to weave in my expertise as a therapist, my empathy as a friend, and my honest humanity as I navigate the difficult terrain of waiting with you.

Many years ago, a friend said to me, "God's plans are always for you, and always beyond you." Through the years, God has deposited in me deep insight and revelation about waiting, and I see now that it wasn't just for me. It was for you as well. I believe you, too, know the pain and the longing for resolution, change, and fulfillment in significant areas of your life.

Several common threads keep us interconnected as human beings. Our shared human experiences are one of those threads, and if we look deeper, we discover that we are woven together by something even more significant. Genesis 1:27 says, "God created mankind in his own image, in the image of

God he created them" (NIV). This means we are connected not only by the experiences we share but also by the God who created us. Our experiences and our pain may look similar or very different, but the feelings are the same when it comes to waiting.

Waiting highlights the ultimate paradox of being made for heaven but finding ourselves on earth. Romans 8:23 says that we "groan inwardly as we wait eagerly" (NIV). The struggle of waiting has an uncanny way of unearthing thoughts, feelings, and reactions in us that not many other things can. It exposes what we believe, challenges our patience, refines our character, and confronts where we've placed our hope. My own story includes the hope, longing, and disappointment that may be familiar to you. And even though some parts sting with lack of closure, I'm committed to offering my imperfect story within these pages.

Our experiences of waiting look and feel different depending on the season of life we're in and who we are in each one. To honor this reality, the devotional weeks follow the unique rhythm of the fall, winter, spring, and summer seasons of our lives. They capture the comingling of expectation and disappointment, fear and hope that ebb and flow. It is meant to be a journey leading to healing and transformation. My hope is that these words will meet you in your current season and help introduce you to the new person you are becoming.

As you enter fall, you may be deeply discouraged. Waiting has taken its toll, and you aren't sure how to keep going. Fall is where you are refined. Your mind, heart, and spirit are collectively evaluating what belongs and what needs to be released.

Winter is a time of solitude, vulnerability, and self-reflection. It is an invitation to bravely venture below the surface and dig deeper than ever. Profound insights that can only be won in winter are rebuilding the person you are becoming.

As you enter spring, you are reemerging, holding fresh hope. Your journey has been hard-fought, and you are still learning how to live into this ever-evolving transformation.

Finally, as you enter summer, you are uncovering renewed youthfulness along with a greater depth of maturity.

The main devotion begins each week, and on the days that follow, prompts encourage you to go deeper—mentally, emotionally, physically, and spiritually. I suggest you write your responses to the prompts in a separate journal. These prompts follow an intentional framework with a different focus for each day:

Day One (You/Soul Care)
Day Two (God)
Day Three (You and God)
Day Four (You and Others)

It is in the tension between our present experiences and our future hopes that we most need a friend. Every word is an extension of my friendship as you navigate the challenging but fruitful terrain of waiting. My deepest hopes are that you would leave different than how you came and that these words would bolster you with the courage to wait well and resurrect hope in every season.

The messages of pain and hope we share with the world are ones we have learned to wrestle with and live out. I wonder what words are being written, what messages are being formed in your life right now as you wait. Your story matters, and it's not for nothing.

I'm cheering you on as you are in the process of becoming the message you will share with the world.

Love,
Barb

There was a man who had four sons.

He wanted his sons to learn not to judge things too quickly. So, he sent them each on a quest, in turn, to go and look at a pear tree that was a great distance away.

The first son went in the winter, the second son went in the spring, the third son went in summer, and the youngest went in fall. When they had all gone and come back, he called them together to describe what they had seen.

The first son said that the tree was very ugly, bent, and twisted.

The second son said no, it was covered with green buds and full of promise.

The third son disagreed; he said it was laden with blossoms that smelled so sweet and looked so beautiful, it was the most graceful thing he had ever seen.

The last son disagreed with all of them; he said it was ripe and drooping with fruit, full of life and fulfilment.

The man then explained to his sons that they were all right, because they had each seen but only one season in the tree's life. He told them that you cannot judge a tree, or a person, by only one season, and that the essence of who they are and the pleasure, joy, and love that comes from that life can only be measured at the end, when all the seasons are up.

If you give up when it is winter, you will miss the promise of your spring, the beauty of your summer and the fulfilment of your fall.[2]

Author unknown

FALL

FALL EMBODIES THE TENSION OF *BOTH, AND.* The world around us bursts with color, while the crispness in the air signals that change is coming. We feel both a relief and a resistance as our pace slows and we prepare for our world to change. Fall is like approaching a yellow light at an intersection. It alerts us to slow down and ready ourselves for change.

Herein lies the tension: We want to hold on to the delight of summer and remain in the nostalgia of fall forever, but with every falling leaf we are invited to learn how to hold beauty and grief in our hearts at the same time. In his book *A Moveable Feast,* Ernest Hemingway observed, "You expected to be sad in the fall. Part of you died each year when the leaves fell from the trees and their branches were bare against the wind and the cold, wintry light. But you knew there would always be the spring, as you knew the river would flow again after it was frozen."[3]

The fall season of waiting is when we learn to release the pain of unfulfilled desires and hold on to our hope and expectation. We have promises and we have longing. We have evidence and we have empty hands. We have joy and we have sorrow. Fall is the in-between. It's the tension-filled place between desire and fulfillment.

In psychology, there is a term known as the *window of tolerance.* Research reveals that it's at the edge of this window—at the cusp of our ability to tolerate the discomfort—where we grow, heal, and change. The *both, and* nature of fall invites us to the cusp of our capacity. It teaches us how to hold competing beliefs and feelings, learning how to honor both and find a new level of hope and acceptance there.

As we observe nature letting go in surrender to the coming winter season, we also learn to release limiting beliefs, distorted thoughts, and all-consuming feelings. As we learn to wait in fall, we realize that some beliefs about our worth and God's character have served as armor to protect our hearts against potential disappointment. In this season we learn to be brave and to release the need to brace for impact. Fall is an invitation into the unexpected freedom that exists in this *both, and* season of our waiting.

It Is *about You*

My darling, everything about you is beautiful,
and there is nothing at all wrong with you.

SONG OF SOLOMON 4:7, NCV

I WALKED IN TO SEE MY THERAPIST, full of grief and grappling with the nos that kept coming my way. I plopped down on her big white chair. "I just feel like it's all about me, like there is something wrong with me."

In her trademark way, she shot back. "Well, it *is* about you." Her response hung in the air.

I'm sure horror covered my face as my fears seemed to be coming true. *Well, there you have it, folks. Even my therapist confirms that it's all my fault.*

Then she smiled. "But not in the way you think."

I dared to raise questioning eyes.

"The reason things haven't worked out *is* about you, but not in the way you think. It's not because something is wrong with you. It's because of all that is right about you. It's because of the quality of who you are that you've waited this long. What is for you must match you, and that takes time."

"No." It's hard to hear that word as anything other than rejection and an indictment of our worth. It reverberates in our minds like a mallet hitting a gong. Formative experiences of rejection scar us, and honestly, they're what keep me in business as a therapist.

In her research on shame, Brené Brown says, "We are psychologically, emotionally, cognitively, and spiritually hardwired for connection, love, and belonging. Connection, along with love and belonging (two expressions of connection), is why we are here, and it is what gives purpose and meaning to our lives."[1]

This hardwiring makes rejection painful. One of the most challenging aspects of waiting is the resounding "no" to something we anticipate with excitement. When we get a no, it's as if someone stuck a pin in a balloon letting the air escape, leaving it deflated and pitiful looking.

After experiencing one of these nos, I remember someone reframing the rejection as protection. *Protection from what?* I didn't see anything wrong with what I wanted or that I needed protection from it. If I was honest, God felt cruel, as if he had gotten my hopes up only to dash them to pieces.

But after the conversation with my therapist, I wondered if God really had been protecting me from circumstances not meant for me. In time, his provision would match how he had made me and the life he had called me to live.

As you challenge the false story that waiting is your fault, you will be free to see previous nos differently and the kind intention behind certain closed doors. The nos are not the end of your story. I believe they are gateways to your yes, to many yeses. Don't allow the nos to whisper lies about you. The waiting is about you, but not in the way you think.

•———— **Day 1 Prompt: Choosing Vulnerability over Shame** ————•

In his book *The Soul of Shame*, Curt Thompson says this:

> We deeply long for connection, to be seen and known for who we are without rejection. But we are terrified of the vulnerability that is required for that very contact. And shame is the variable that mediates that fear of rejection in the face of vulnerability. But in the Trinity we see something that we must pay attention to: God does not leave. The loving relationship shared between Father, Son and Spirit is the ground on which all other models of life and creativity rest. In this relationship of constant self-giving, vulnerable and joyful love, *shame has no oxygen to breathe.*[2]

In our longings for connection and fears of rejection, the truth that "God does not leave" has power to allay our fears and dispel our shame.

Living It Out 🌿 Consider how you can begin interpreting the nos and delays through a lens of love rather than neglect. Write down what comes to mind.

———— Day 2 Prompt: Reconciling God and Waiting ————

Reconciling God as good and kind with the pain of our circumstances can be challenging. In *My Utmost for His Highest*, Oswald Chambers references Luke 11:11-13, where Jesus is talking about fatherhood.

> There are times when your Father will appear as if He were an unnatural father—as if He were callous and indifferent—but remember, He is not. "Everyone who asks receives" (Luke 11:10). If all you see is a shadow on the face of the Father right now, hang on to the fact that He will ultimately give you clear understanding and will fully justify Himself in everything that He has allowed into your life.[3]

Living It Out 🌿 How have you struggled to reconcile pain with a kind and loving God? Write down what stands out to you in the quote.

———— Day 3 Prompt: Choosing Right over Wrong ————

It can be healing to realize the nos are because of what is *right* about you.

Have you been tempted to believe you're waiting because of something that's wrong with you? Consider the Old Testament stories of Joseph, David, and Abraham. They waited much longer than they imagined for promises to be fulfilled. Joseph waited thirteen years for his dream to come to pass, David waited about twenty-two years to be recognized as king, and Abraham waited twenty-five years to hold his promised child.

It's possible they looked inward and questioned whether the delay was because something was wrong with them. In reality, God's infinite love for them was at the heart of the delay.

Living It Out 🌿 Pray and invite God into this struggle. Ask him to show you all that is right about you, and how this truth is at the heart of the delay.

Day 4 Prompt: Trusted Community

In 1912, French sociologist Émile Durkheim introduced the term *collective effervescence*,[4] the experience of connection, communal emotion, and a "sensation of sacredness"[5] that happens when we are part of something bigger than ourselves. Durkheim also proposed that during collective effervescence our focus shifts from ourselves to others.

Powerful changes take place in us when we wrestle with our questions and pain within a trusted community. In this "sensation of sacredness," we remember there are purposes in our waiting that extend far beyond us. We aren't alone or to blame, and although we aren't privy to how God is providing for us, he is still worthy of our trust and confidence.

> Share each other's burdens, and in this way obey the law of Christ.
> GALATIANS 6:2, NLT

Living It Out 🌿 Reflect on a time when you shared your burdens with someone you trust, or they shared theirs with you. Remember how this helped you feel less alone and more connected to them and to God.

Hidden Treasure

*If we wait in the conviction that a seed has been planted
and that something has already begun, it changes the way we wait.*
HENRI NOUWEN

WHEN I LOOK UP THE DEFINITION for the word *wait*,[1] this is what I find:

to *stay in place* in *expectation* of
to *remain stationary* in *readiness* or expectation
to *pause* for another to catch up
to *look forward* expectantly
to *hold back* expectantly
a *hidden or concealed position*
a *state or attitude* of watchfulness and expectancy

What I notice about each definition is our power to choose. *Staying in place, pausing, looking forward, holding back* all reflect choices we make. At some point, we may have believed that to wait was to be passive and powerless. But I don't see passivity or powerlessness anywhere in these descriptions. Instead, I see courage, bravery, vulnerability, acceptance, surrender, and hope.

The description I never saw before but that resonates deeply is a *hidden or concealed position.* We often mistake being hidden for being unseen, and this mislabeling reinforces the lie that we aren't valuable.

In Matthew 13:44 Jesus says, "Heaven's kingdom realm can be illustrated like this: A person discovered that there was hidden treasure in a field. Upon finding it, he hid it again. Because of uncovering such treasure, he was overjoyed and sold all that he possessed to buy the entire field just so he could have the treasure."

The treasure's hidden state didn't depreciate its value; rather, the person hid the treasure again *because* it was so valuable. He sold everything to buy the field just because it contained the hidden treasure.

Though hidden, the treasure wasn't unseen. And the person who discovered it was anything but passive and powerless. Although this verse speaks to our value to Jesus and the sacrifice he made for our salvation, I also believe it communicates truths that extend into other areas of life, including waiting seasons.

We have infinite value to God, and what matters to us matters to him. Who we are and what we hope for are like hidden treasures, and in our waiting, we are not only discovering our value but also learning how to partner with God in faith.

We come to God in faith knowing that he is real and that he rewards the faith of those who passionately seek him.
HEBREWS 11:6

Shifting your mindset from passivity and powerlessness to empowered participation with God will transform you and the way you move through your seasons of waiting. May you be convinced of your worthiness and choose to believe you are seen by God, even in hiddenness.

Day 1 Prompt: Finding Your Agency

During my counseling sessions, I use the word *agency* a lot. According to psychologist Albert Bandura, agency is defined as "the human capability to influence one's functioning and the course of events by one's actions."[2]

Bandura suggests there are four functions of agency: the ability to set intentions, the ability to have forethought, the capacity to self-regulate, and the ability to self-reflect.[3]

A lack of agency is like the old "chicken and the egg" adage. It's hard to know which one came first—limiting beliefs or painful experiences. Either way, the pain of both is detrimental to us.

Living It Out 🌿 Do you struggle to embrace your sense of agency? What has led you to feel powerless: Circumstances that feel out of your control? The daily weight of unfulfilled desires? Write down any limiting belief you may have, as well as a quote, verse, or prayer that reminds you of the agency God wants you to embrace.

———— Day 2 Prompt: The Seeds of Waiting ————

Have you been feeling hidden—like you were walking around in the dark? When we consider the conditions in which seeds grow, they are first planted in a concealed, dark place. In John 12:24 Jesus says, "A single grain of wheat will never be more than a single grain of wheat unless it drops into the ground and dies. Because then it sprouts and produces a great harvest of wheat."

According to Chong Singsit, a biotechnologist, "The endosperm [contained in the seed] must die and give up its contents in order to support life [and] regenerate the dying seed. If the endosperm refuses to give up itself and support the developing embryo, there could not be a new life springing up from the dying seed."[4]

Being hidden is painful, and it's hard to imagine life springing from this obscurity. But as you keep choosing surrender, deep transformation is happening in you.

Living It Out 🌿 Reflect on this example and ask God to illuminate the transformation taking place in you.

———— Day 3 Prompt: The Problem with Slowing Down ————

Pausing, remaining stationary, staying in place, and *holding back* can be difficult. The other day at the drug store, the cashier rushed to apologize to the customer in front of me for the three-second wait they had to endure. How impatient has our society become if we feel slighted by the briefest delay and those serving us feel obligated to profusely apologize for these "inconveniences"? The world around us has influenced this difficulty to slow down and wait.

Living It Out 🌿 How can you reclaim the beauty of slow and stationary living? Notice how pausing, being stationary, and holding back for even a few moments can help redefine this challenging part of waiting.

• ———————— **Day 4 Prompt: Looking for Other Seeds** ————————— •

If we follow the analogy of the seed from Day 2, we see that although each seed is buried alone, many other seeds have been buried too. The juxtaposition here is that the seed is both alone and not alone, since many other seeds are undergoing the same process.

Waiting is part of the human experience, both personal and collective. In one season, we may wait for restoration in a relationship, and in another, for healing of mind and body. Each person, like a single seed, knows what it is to wait, making up a collective human experience we can all relate to.

Living It Out 🌿 Who are the other "seeds" in your life undergoing different versions of the season you're walking through? Do you have a friend who is waiting for a baby? A parent who is waiting for physical healing? A sibling who is waiting for a spouse, or a spouse who is waiting for direction? Reach out to one of these people this week. Let them know you see them, and allow space for both of you to share about your personal seed-like experiences.

The Stories We Tell Ourselves

These seasons of suffering are not for nothing. They will grow you.
They will shape you. They will soften you. They will allow
you to experience God's comfort and compassion.

LYSA TERKEURST, *IT'S NOT SUPPOSED TO BE THIS WAY*

ONE OF THE REASONS we anxiously ruminate on a thought is because we are trying to "close the loop" and resolve our stories.

It reminds me of when someone is playing the piano, and the song seems to end on a note that leaves the audience in a suspended state. *Resolution* in music happens when the musician moves from a note of dissonance to consonance (a final or stable-sounding one). It's not until the pianist hits the final sounding note that our ears can rest, and we feel satisfied as the melody resolves.

When we're waiting, it's as if we were existing within that suspended state. We're longing for the note that brings resolution to our stories. The stories we tell ourselves about our stories will keep us either ruminating or moving toward resolution. In my work as a therapist, so much of what I do revolves around shining a light on these stories and helping clients engage them with curiosity and compassion.

Brené Brown says, "Storytelling helps us all impose order on chaos—including emotional chaos. When we're in pain, we create a narrative to help us make sense of it. This story doesn't have to be based on any real information. . . . This unconscious storytelling leaves us stuck."[1]

The pain of waiting compels us to fabricate stories to ease the discomfort we feel. If you're waiting for direction, financial breakthrough, physical or emotional healing, a restored relationship, a baby, a job, or a spouse, what stories have you been telling yourself about it? Perhaps stories about your worth, God's character, and the probability that God would *want* to come through for you.

In Matthew 8:1-3, a man with leprosy approaches Jesus for healing.

> After [Jesus] came down from teaching on the hillside, massive crowds began following him. Suddenly, a leper walked up to Jesus and threw himself down before him in worship and said, "Lord, you have the power to heal me . . . *if you really want to.*" Jesus reached out his hand and touched the leper and said, "Of course I want to heal you—be healed!" And instantly, all signs of leprosy disappeared!

This man didn't question God's ability, but rather his desire. This gives us insight into the stories the man was most likely telling himself: Stories that cast doubt on God's kindness, and whether he cared to heal him. Stories about whether he was worth finding an audience with God. We need to pay attention to the questions we ask, because they reveal the stories we tell ourselves too.

Jesus allayed this man's fears by saying, "Of course I want to heal you." This was Jesus' gentle way of correcting the stories the man had been telling himself.

We can rest within what's true about God and ourselves. God cares, and even now he is drawing near to answer your questions and gently correct any false narratives so the stories you tell yourself reflect his *willing* heart of love towards you.

•——————— Day 1 Prompt: Expanding Our Stories ———————•

One story that may surface when you're in pain is "If I can just understand what is happening in my life and why, then it will hurt less." Putting your experiences into their proper context does hold value. However, this story is limiting because it suggests that understanding is the only suitable remedy to alleviate your pain. How can you expand this story to include important details that may have been left out?

Living It Out 🌿 In your journal, write down the story you've been rehearsing about your waiting experience, and then write down the new and expansive one you've discovered (or want to discover).

●————— Day 2 Prompt: God's Desire or Ability —————●

The man with leprosy in Matthew 8 revealed his doubts about Jesus' *desire* to heal him. We don't read about him doubting Jesus' ability, but if you listen closely, the third voice in his conversation with Jesus is, "I'm not sure if your power is personal."

You may carry doubts about whether God is able to come through for you, or you may question if God wants to. Or perhaps you believe God is able to come through for everyone but you. What have your doubts centered on?

Living It Out 🌿 Read the story in Matthew 8. Notice how Jesus addresses the man's doubts, and consider how Jesus wants to approach the doubts you have been carrying.

●————— Day 3 Prompt: Taking Inventory —————●

I've found one practice particularly helpful in challenging the stories that circulate in our minds: In your journal, draw one column and write down all the things you are afraid of. In the second column, write everything you know to be true as it relates to that fear. For example, you might fear the uncertainties that come with waiting, so in the next column, remind yourself of what you do know and are certain of. Or you might fear a conflict with a loved one, so in the next column, recall the responsibilities you have taken to repair the relationship and any outstanding opportunities that may belong to you.

Living It Out 🌿 After you have written down your fears and truths, notice how aligning your heart with the truths helps shift your perspective and provides relief from your worries.

⸺ Day 4 Prompt: The Power of Sharing Our Stories ⸺

Did you know that sharing stories with one another activates parts of the brain that deepen connection? An article titled "The Science of Storytelling: What Listening to a Story Does to Our Brains" discusses how the brains of the storyteller and the listener synchronize. Listening to a story activates the listener's brain in a way that turns the story into their own experience.

When we hear a story, not only are the language processing parts in our brains activated, but also any other area in our brains that we would use when experiencing the events of the story. This research helps to confirm the experiences we have all had when sharing our stories with someone we trust. We feel seen, understood, and less alone.[2]

Living It Out 🌿 Identify someone you trust to share the story you have been carrying about God's desire or ability. Allow this act of storytelling to relieve your heart of loneliness and provide the connection you need.

Hidden, Not *Unseen*

When [God] calls a soul simultaneously to greatness and obscurity,
the fruit—if we wait for it—can change the world.

ALICIA BRITT CHOLE,

ANONYMOUS: JESUS' HIDDEN YEARS . . . AND YOURS

WAITING INVOLVES HIDDENNESS.

Part of our hardwiring as human beings is the compelling need to uncover what's hidden. We are passionate about exposing injustice or displaying something noteworthy. We only like mystery if we can solve it, and we feel frustrated when we aren't able to figure it out.

If waiting involves hiddenness, then hiddenness involves mystery.

When our future is hidden, we feel afraid. When God seems hidden, we feel hurt. We wait for hidden things to come to light, and we grow more discouraged with every day that passes with no change.

According to psychoanalyst Sigmund Freud, *projection* is a defense mechanism that serves to protect us against the fear of the unknown.[1] This fear projects a false reality about our futures and compels us to create stories to make sense of what we don't understand.

Projection is a deeply human strategy. We make up stories to make meaning out of our lives. Fear at the root of projection distracts us from connecting with a greater reality—one anchored in love rather than fear.

Consider what goes into a successful surprise party. The element of surprise hinges on everyone's ability to keep the secret. Love and generosity are the motivators behind keeping the details hidden, and we feel enormous success when the guest of honor is actually surprised.

Proverbs 25:2 says, "It is the glory of God to conceal a matter, but the glory of kings is to search out a matter" (NASB). Just as the host is diligent about concealing the surprise, "God's privilege" (NLT) is to conceal the "matter" (various translations). It's his glory to conceal because it's his glory to reveal.

What if there is a proper time for certain matters in your life to be revealed—similar to the moment you think you're going to a romantic dinner for two but instead find everyone shouting "Happy birthday" at your surprise party?

God's reveal for you happens at the time he knows you will receive the most joy and fulfillment. The waiting, hiddenness, and mystery are necessary to ultimately give you something precious. This truth intercepts fearful projections of a future filled with lack.

What "matter" are you waiting for? What area feels hidden and enveloped in mystery? As you acknowledge God's extravagant love behind the hiddenness, notice your heart softening and your hands relaxing their grip. Hold this truth close: God is not withholding from you. He only conceals so he can reveal, and he is waiting to give you all that he has prepared for you.

• —— Day 1 Prompt: Getting Comfortable with the Unknown —— •

So far no one has been able to successfully throw me a surprise party. It's not because my friends or family aren't skilled secret keepers; it's because I'm too nosy. The irony is that I love surprises. Why then do I let my inquisitive nature get the best of me? My best guess is that it's one part curiosity and one part control.

Our fears of the unknown trigger us to maintain control over our lives. God constantly invites us to release control and step with him into the mystery. Every time we accept his invitation, our faith deepens and our capacity for the unknown grows.

Living It Out 🌿 Recall a time you organized or were the recipient of a surprise party. How can this experience bring insights to your feelings about the unknown? Journal what comes to mind.

—————— **Day 2 Prompt: Get Specific** ——————

Did you know that the phrase "Fear not" is repeated in the Bible 365 times?[2] God repeats this refrain once for every day of the year because he knows how tempted we are to fear.

Don't settle for vague language regarding how you feel. Ask yourself, *What specifically am I afraid of as I navigate hiddenness? Am I afraid of future loss, being forgotten or abandoned?* The more specific your language, the more targeted you can be in conversations with God.

God doesn't want you to be in the dark about your feelings. He wants to illuminate your mind and heart so you can bring everything to him.

Living It Out 🌿 Write down what you fear about hiddenness. Offer what you've written to God, noticing what he says or gives you in exchange.

—————— **Day 3 Prompt: Remaining Faithful in Obscurity** ——————

Fear creeps in when we believe our hiddenness is synonymous with being unseen. Before David reigned as king over Israel, he worked as a humble shepherd boy in his father's fields. He was faithful in obscurity because he knew that, although hidden to others, he was fully seen by God.

Richard Rohr says,

> Faith is a kind of knowing that doesn't need to know for certain and yet doesn't dismiss knowledge either. With faith, we don't need to obtain or hold all knowledge because we know that we are being held inside a Much Larger Frame and Perspective.[3]

As Paul puts it, "Now we see in a mirror dimly, but then face to face. Now I know in part; then I shall know fully, even as I have been fully known" (1 Corinthians 13:12, ESV).

David knew he was "being held inside a Much Larger Frame." His confidence in God helped him see purpose in and beyond hiddenness.

Living It Out 🌿 Write down what hiddenness has felt like and how you might see it differently when you consider the life of David and this quote from Richard Rohr.

•———— **Day 4 Prompt: The Fruit that Changes the World** ————•

Do you ever ask God to give you a word that you can apply to the new year? One time mine was *discipline*, and for obvious reasons, I was nervous what it meant for the year ahead. It came from Hebrews 12:11, which says, "For the time being no discipline brings joy, but seems sad and painful; yet to those who have been trained by it, afterwards it yields the peaceful fruit of righteousness" (AMP).

The following year my word was *fruit*. It's from the same verse in Hebrews and reminds me of a quote from Alicia Britt Chole: "When [God] calls a soul simultaneously to greatness and obscurity, the fruit—if we wait for it—can change the world."[4] Fruit grows from the painful work of discipline and trusting God when we have no evidence that doing so is worthwhile.

Living It Out 🌿 Waiting is its own form of discipline. The challenges of waiting inevitably grow us; or spiritually speaking, waiting yields fruit in our lives. What fruit has waiting yielded in you: The fruit of the Spirit: "love, joy, peace, patience, kindness, goodness, faithfulness, gentleness, and self-control (Galatians 5:22, NLT)? Perhaps specific fruit in your relationships, career, etc.? Reflect on how these fruits have the power to "change the world."

Hope deferred makes the
heart sick, but a dream
fulfilled is a tree of life.

Proverbs 13:12, NLT

Getting beyond the Boxes

*Waiting on God requires the willingness to bear uncertainty,
to carry within oneself the unanswered question, lifting the heart
to God about it whenever it intrudes upon one's thoughts.*

ELISABETH ELLIOT, *PASSION AND PURITY*

BINARY THINKING IS TEMPTING, especially while we're waiting. All of us are familiar with that either-or and black-and-white perspective that we believe gives us a sense of safety and control. In actuality, these binary boxes leave us emptied of peace and full of anxiety.

We feel the push and pull between being resigned *or* hopeful, passive *or* active, despairing *or* believing, anxious *or* avoidant, connected *or* disconnected, forgotten *or* remembered. I encourage clients to consider how this either-or thinking might be creating more distress than it's relieving. And I explain how it eliminates the curiosity necessary to account for life's complexities. The appeal, however, is that binary thinking mitigates the tension surrounding contrasting feelings and realities.

Whenever I took steps toward my desires and was met with disappointment, I quickly plummeted from hope to despair. It seemed impossible to feel disappointed while also remaining hopeful. I thought I had to choose, because I didn't know how these experiences could coexist.

When we consider the stories in the Bible, we see how many of the characters were learning to hold opposing feelings and experiences as they waited on God.

David is a perfect example. He was anointed king while he was still a shepherd boy. He was called to sit on a king's throne, but for about seven years he lived in a cave as an outlaw. Joseph had a similar story. He was given dreams about reigning over his brothers. But these dreams seemed to lead him further away from promotion, as his brothers sold him into slavery, and later he was shipped off to prison. In light of David's and Joseph's stories and what we know about our own, we may wonder, *How did they, and how can I, continue to acknowledge God's promises alongside the pain of current circumstances?*

There is no magic formula. The way to hold both the pain of waiting *and* the hope of God's promises is through daily choices to trust God in view of our pain, not in spite of it. We love the Psalms because David was both a fugitive and a king, a man with flaws and "a man after [God's] own heart" (1 Samuel 13:14, NLT). His songs teach us how to pour out our fears while also declaring our trust in God.

Each decision to trust God creates new paths in our minds to better hold the complexities of life. This is the path of integration. Psychology professor Michelle Buck says, "Wholeness is about embracing, not denying, all of our feelings."[1] This wholeness accounts for the pain of your waiting *and* the truth that God is still working. What anchored men like David and Joseph during their seasons of waiting is what anchors us now—the continual decision to rely on God no matter the conditions.

Day 1 Prompt: Leaving Space for Mystery

It's important to leave space in our faith for mystery. As "people of faith," we can become so obsessed with certainty that we forget Scripture refers to us as "stewards of the mysteries of God" (1 Corinthians 1:4, NASB).

Waiting is full of mystery, and it will feel unbearable if we approach it with an obsession for certainty. As you leave room for mystery, something transformative happens—you are strengthened to bear uncertainty with courage.

Living It Out 🌿 What other mysteries in life can teach you how to hold mystery in this season? Perhaps how a baby grows in its mother's womb? Or the chemistry that makes it possible for two people to fall in love? Reflect on either of these situations, and write down what comes to mind.

Day 2 Prompt: A New Way

Jesus lived in a culture steeped in legalism—*the excessive adherence to the traditions of men instead of God's perfect law of love.* Talk about binary boxes. Jesus blew up every box the Pharisees (religious people) tried to put him in.

In Mark 2, we see a perfect example of Jesus introducing a new way. Jesus and his disciples are hungry and decide to pluck "heads of grain" (Matthew 12:1) in a field on the Sabbath. The Pharisees rebuke Jesus and his disciples for doing what was considered "work" on the Sabbath, until Jesus flips the script and says, "The Sabbath was made for man, not man for the Sabbath" (Mark 2:27, NIV).

Living It Out 🌿 What old "box" is Jesus inviting you to do away with? And what new way is he introducing to you? Reflect and journal what comes to mind.

Day 3 Prompt: Imagining Life outside the Boxes

It can be an exercise in vulnerability to ask curious questions about another person's life. Perhaps because I ask questions for a living, I notice how difficult curiosity can be for so many.

My friend Elizabeth is one of the most intentional question-askers, and it's one of the aspects I appreciate most about our friendship. When someone we trust asks us questions, it helps us imagine life outside of the box we might be living in. Questions are powerful because they help us discover a new perspective, and while we're waiting, perspective is a priceless gift.

In the Gospels, Jesus asked 307 questions.[2] Clearly, Jesus knew how questions help challenge our status quo and encourage us to go deeper.

Living It Out 🌿 Recall a time someone asked intentional questions that expanded your perspective. Write down how these questions impacted you and how you can practice asking questions of yourself.

—————— Day 4 Prompt: A Wholehearted Life ——————

I admire how my therapist brings her whole self into the room. When I met her for the first time, it was 7:30 a.m., and she was passionately vacuuming the waiting room. She turned off the vacuum and in her enthusiastic way said, "Oh, hi! I'm Laura. You must be Barb!"

She set the vacuum aside, directed me to her room, followed me in, and closed the door. Then she kicked off her shoes, threw her legs across her chair, and said, "Okay, tell me about yourself." I was floored in the best way. As a therapist myself, I was inspired by her authenticity.

She showed me the freedom of ditching the boxes, and she modeled wholehearted living, which impacts how we approach waiting. If we feel sad, we allow ourselves to express sadness. If we feel disappointed, we can express disappointment without abandoning hope.

Living It Out 🌿 Who has shown you how to live wholeheartedly? Reflect and write down who comes to mind and how their influence has impacted you.

Learning Our Purpose

In this season God intends to give us an unshakable identity in Him,
that no amount of adoration nor rejection can alter.

ALICIA BRITT CHOLE,
ANONYMOUS: JESUS' HIDDEN YEARS . . . AND YOURS

I DIDN'T ALWAYS KNOW I WANTED TO BE A THERAPIST. Like many others, I felt pressure to know exactly what I was supposed to do in life, as quickly as possible. Society places a strong emphasis on knowing our purpose without first accounting for the time it takes to learn what we're passionate about and where to channel those passions.

Identity and purpose are intertwined, and sometimes we can push people to know their purpose before they have had the proper chance to learn their identity. Doing so creates confusion and anxiety because it's impossible to discern our purpose if we have no clue who we are. Learning our identity is a process involving intention, time, experience, and space to unfold.

When I graduated from high school, I thought I would work as a nurse and missionary in an underdeveloped country. But life didn't exactly pan out that way. My first job after Bible college was at a teaching hospital in Baltimore as an administrative assistant. Next I spent a couple of years in the corporate world, and after that I moved to Africa as a missionary and then back to Baltimore with no idea what I was "supposed" to do next. For practical reasons, I enrolled in an esthetics program, and after working in the beauty industry for two years, I finally had my big epiphany about being a therapist.

Every life transition involves waiting and unknowns. Any light bulb moments we have about our purpose and the form it will take result from difficult moments of waiting.

It's in this waiting and looking to God for our purpose that we learn who we are. As we grow in our identity, our purpose comes into focus. It reminds me of adjusting a camera to bring the picture into focus. As you and I discover more about ourselves, our purpose is clarified.

This "bringing our purpose into focus" isn't a one-and-done experience. It ebbs and flows through seasons of life. I believe certain foundational aspects of our purpose are fixed, like loving others or growing deeper with God. But other aspects of our purpose develop and change. Take the field of medicine, for example. The foundational purpose in medicine is to heal sick people's bodies, but the outworking of how to do this most effectively has changed over time.

I discovered that my foundational purpose was to help others become more whole versions of themselves, but how I live out that purpose has changed many times. As you discover the varied forms your purpose will take, don't be surprised when you face waiting and unknowns along the way. Be encouraged as you wait for your purpose to come into focus, knowing you are discovering who God created you to be. The fall seasons of waiting spur you on to root deeper in your identity, and empower you to discover the manifold purposes for your life.

Day 1 Prompt: Uncovering Your Identity

I remember one of my clients expressing frustration about not knowing their purpose. They realized they never felt free to discover their identity because it had been *assigned* to them by others at an early age.

This client's insight highlights how identity and purpose ask two very different questions.

Identity: *"Who am I?"*
Purpose: *"What am I meant to do?"*

Answering the identity question can feel scary because it requires that we journey into uncharted territory within ourselves, possibly parts of ourselves we have resisted getting to know.

Living It Out 🌿 We need a solid place to begin answering this identity question. The statements below are a great foundation to build on as you consider what is true about who you are.

You are *deeply loved.*
You are *worthy.*
You are *enough.*
You *belong.*

•——— **Day 2 Prompt: An Essential Ingredient to Waiting** ———•

Flexibility is an essential ingredient in waiting. I recall a time I tried baking cookies for a friend. I put the ingredients together, popped the dough in the oven, and waited while they baked to perfection.

But when I opened the oven, I was horrified to see what looked more like burnt pancakes than cookies. My friend and I laughed when we realized I'd forgotten to add baking soda to the batter.

Flexibility is to waiting, what baking soda is to cookies. It may sound like an odd correlation, but if we are going to navigate the twists and turns of waiting well, we need to stay flexible. Waiting without flexibility leads to feeling burned out—just like my poor cookies.

Living It Out 🌿 Reflect on what waiting with flexibility has been like (or could be like), and what waiting without flexibility has been like. Write down what comes to mind.

•——— **Day 3 Prompt: The Many Versions of Our Purpose** ———•

It can feel monumental to realize there can be many ways to live out your purpose.

Although the context is different, it makes me think of the many versions of the Bible. In English alone, there are more than 450 versions.[1] A verse in the King James Version reads very differently than in the New Living Translation or *The Message*. They are all connected to the same original sources, but the way they communicate them is different.

Understanding your purpose can feel like this. You can learn a new aspect of yourself with each new version you experience. Waiting to discover new facets of your purpose will be challenging but worth your time, effort, and commitment.

Living It Out 🌿 What versions of your purpose have you experienced so far? How have they helped you better understand your identity? How can these experiences encourage you to trust God in your current season? Reflect and write what comes to mind.

Day 4 Prompt: Our Words Matter

My friend Becky was one of the first people to encourage my passion for writing. She never missed an opportunity to share my early blog posts with others and tell me how much she was touched by them. Her words meant more to me than she knows. Her encouragement communicated that the words I shared mattered to others.

As we walk alongside each other, let's remember our words have the power to catapult people into their purpose.

Living It Out 🌿 Whose words have encouraged you? How did they boost your courage as you waited for your purpose to come into focus? Who can you encourage in this way? Write down who comes to mind.

When Hope Feels Complicated

Hope stands up to its knees in the past and keeps its eyes on the future.
FREDERICK BUECHNER, *A ROOM CALLED REMEMBER*

I READ A QUOTE ON SOCIAL MEDIA from Vienna Pharaon, a licensed marriage and family therapist, who said, "When I know I am deserving, when I know I am lovable, when I know I am good enough, I no longer need to wait for an outcome to determine that for me."[1]

A couple of years ago I had a conversation with two close friends about a risk I was terrified to take. I felt caught between hope and potential disappointment. No matter how much I analyzed it, I couldn't see a way to mitigate the risk and guarantee a positive outcome. Hope felt complicated.

Before we experience painful disappointment, our hope seems simple, even easy, as it is for children. Expecting good things feels natural to them, and they don't spend precious time imagining the ways life could go wrong.

My friends helped me see how the pain of waiting and the sting of past disappointment were controlling my willingness to take risks. The unconscious narrative fueling my fear centered on outcomes: If the outcome turned out as I wanted, then the risk was worth taking. I was controlled by *past pain* and by *future outcomes.*

The most dangerous part was that my worth was tied up in this fear. If the outcome didn't turn out well, then I would deem the risk not worth taking and myself not worthwhile. No wonder the fear was overwhelming.

I love the quote from Vienna Pharaon because it detaches our worth from outcomes. Life presents us with many opportunities to take risks, and each one will feel impossible if we attach our value to it.

A turning point comes when we realize that taking the risk *is* the win, and that each risk is for us, not for an outcome. When we step out in faith, we partner with hope and build our confidence. We experience our capability to take risks despite everything we've been through. It's a bold act of courage to choose hope anyway.

This is audacious living—choosing to defy fear that tries to control us. This is the power of acceptance—acknowledging reality while maintaining hope for a different future.

Jesus said, "No one can take my life from me. I sacrifice it voluntarily. For I have the authority to lay it down when I want to and also to take it up again" (John 10:18, NLT). Jesus risked the Cross in view of its pain. He knew who he was and that he was called to lay down his life out of the conviction of his Sonship and his mission to restore humanity to himself. And yet as a human, he also knew the tremendous pain it would bring (note the agony he experienced at Gethsemane [Matthew 26:36-46; Luke 22:39-46]). Jesus held the hope of what the Cross would accomplish alongside the reality that he would endure its temporary pain.

Let's frame risks differently by choosing a hope that believes our worthiness and the conviction of our purpose. In doing so, we can be confident regardless of the outcome.

•——— Day 1 Prompt: The Trap of Overanalyzing ———•

A friend once told me she almost bought a T-shirt for me that said, "Hold on, let me overanalyze that." We laughed because we both know me well. Analyzing is one of those "two sides of the same coin" traits. On one side, my analytical eye helps me sift through my clients' thoughts and feelings for important patterns. On the other side, it can keep me circling a situation like a frazzled hamster on a wheel.

Living It Out 🌿 When thinking is no longer productive, move your body. Physical activity helps release the fear that keeps you circling. Close your eyes and imagine putting whatever you have been overanalyzing in a box on a shelf until you're ready to revisit the idea. In the meantime, go for a walk or engage in whatever form of movement feels restorative. This energy shift generates more clarity on the situation because you will be approaching it with fresh eyes and from a more embodied place.

Day 2 Prompt: Declaration of Identity

I believe there is something important for us in the words spoken over Jesus at the commencement of his public ministry. Matthew 3:17 says, "Suddenly the voice of the Father shouted from the sky, saying, 'This is my Son—the Beloved! My greatest delight is in him.'"

This powerful declaration from heaven affirmed Jesus' identity. Jesus knew who he was and who he belonged to. Knowing who we are and who we belong to empowers us to face our fears with courage.

Living It Out 🌿 Have you been feeling unsure about who you are? What words of love would Jesus speak over you: That there is no flaw in you (Song of Solomon 4:7)? That you are fearfully and wonderfully made (Psalm 139:14)? Read these verses; then write what comes to mind so you can repeat it to yourself this week.

Day 3 Prompt: Success versus Fruitfulness

Our society is obsessed with outcomes. We quantify everything as a benchmark for worthiness. A friend once shared how difficult it is to do anything unless it's quantifiable, including a walk outside. I remember asking, "Can't you just take a leisurely stroll and enjoy being outside?" They responded with an emphatic no and said they measure everything because it makes them feel more accomplished.

When I think of outcomes, I think of success. Henri Nouwen says this about the difference between success and fruitfulness:

> There is a great difference between successfulness and fruitfulness. . . .
> A successful person has the energy to create something, to keep
> control over its development. . . . Fruits, however, come from

weakness and vulnerability. . . . A child is the fruit conceived in vulnerability, community is the fruit born through shared brokenness, and intimacy is the fruit that grows through touching one another's wounds.[2]

Living It Out 🌿 Reflect on the following statement, writing down what comes to mind: Success is based on positive outcomes, but fruitfulness extends beyond outcomes and grows even out of difficult and imperfect situations.

——— Day 4 Prompt: The Power of Conversation ———

Conversations with people you trust will always spark important realizations, as they did with my two friends from this week's devotional.

I read a quote recently that says,

> Good conversations are kinetic and collaborative—they are much like pieces of symphonic music where everyone must contribute to the harmony and rhythm. . . . Sometimes you have a latent insight you don't even know you have, and can't articulate, and then someone says something that unearths it and you feel a light bulb go off in your head. . . . Conversation can be an incredibly creative endeavor.[3]

Living It Out 🌿 Who can you have a conversation with to bring understanding to your current circumstances?

Taking It Out on God

I spill out my heart to you and tell you all my troubles.

PSALM 142:2

AT THE END OF 2019, I reached a place in my waiting that felt different. I was angry and found myself dealing with it in an unfamiliar way. Instead of pursuing God, I withdrew from him. I washed my hands and threw in the towel, and to show God how serious I was, I iced him out of my life.

During this time, a friend sat with me in the corner of a local coffee shop, and I shared my anger while Bruno Mars serenaded us in the background. I looked down as I wrapped my hands around the warm coffee cup, hoping it would bring solace to my weary heart. As I drowned my sorrows at the bottom of an eight-dollar latte, my friend asked if I knew about those movie scenes where a woman is so hurt that she explodes in anger at the man she loves. After screaming and punching his chest, she collapses into his arms, sobbing.

"*That* is the place you need to get to with God," my friend said. "You need to believe he is secure enough to handle the full weight of your anger and disappointment. You need to feel so close to God that you can scream and punch his chest in anger until you melt into his arms, sobbing."

This picture resonated deeply.

I'm not sure which was harder for me—unleashing my anger on God or melting into his arms, sobbing. I hadn't done either. Instead, I had softened the edges of my anger to make it more palatable for God, and when things didn't change, I turned away in resentment. By withdrawing *from* God, I had revealed a deficiency in my understanding *of* God. I didn't believe our relationship was secure enough to unleash something so raw. I didn't believe

God's love was strong enough to take my punches and hold me while I sobbed. What was also difficult to reckon with was that *I* wasn't secure enough to do any of these things with God.

Maybe you can relate. Formative experiences in our upbringings inform how we show up with God in these moments. How our parents related to us when we felt "big" emotions greatly influences us as adults. For example, expressing anger and receiving anger in return and hearing our sadness met with dismissive remarks were moments of emotional impact.

Mark Nepo, in his devotional *The Book of Awakening*, says, "It doesn't take very long for each of us to accumulate an emotional history. A child burns her hand on a stove and a fear of fire begins; in a tender moment, a hand is slapped and a fear of love begins. Our emotional associations and reflexes run deep."[1]

Withdrawing from God in anger reveals a need to grow in security within ourselves and with him. First Peter 5:7 reads, "Casting all your care upon Him, for He cares for you" (NKJV), but many other Bible translations use words like *throw, give, turn over*, and *pour out* to describe this casting of your cares onto God. Take the word you need today as permission to unfurl your heart to God. Allow this casting, throwing, giving, turning over, or pouring out to relieve your pain and deepen your security.

•——— Day 1 Prompt: Identifying Your Attachment Style ———•

Some additional context that will help us understand our responses involves attachment styles. Attachment theory was developed by Mary Ainsworth and John Bowlby in the 1950s. Bowlby defines attachment as a "lasting psychological connectedness between human beings."[2]

I could fill hundreds of pages with commentary on attachment styles, but here's a simple description for each one:

Anxious Attachment *abandons* self.
Avoidant Attachment *preserves* self.
Anxious-Avoidant *sabotages* self.
Secure Attachment *honors* self and others.

Waiting will not only expose our emotions and inner dialogue but also put us face-to-face with our attachment style.

Living It Out 🌿 When you are in pain from waiting, are you more likely to *abandon, preserve, sabotage,* or *honor* yourself? Reflect and write down which attachment style resonates with you.

● ──────── **Day 2 Prompt: Your History with God** ──────── ●

When a movie character has a pivotal moment of reflection about a certain person and memories replay in their mind, usually these flashes put their relationship into perspective and prompt them to significant action.

I had a similar moment the first time I heard the song "History" from Maverick City Music. The idea that God and I had a history never occurred to me. Flashes of memories reminded me of pivotal moments with him. Pain had skewed my perspective of God's heart, but as I remembered our history, my heart underwent important adjustments.

Living It Out 🌿 Listen to the song "History" from Maverick City Music, and reflect on your history with God: when he protected and provided for you and when he was faithful, gracious, and loving to you. As you remember, ask God to make the necessary adjustments in your heart.

● ──────── **Day 3 Prompt: Growing in Awareness** ──────── ●

Awareness does not create change as much as it creates the necessary environment for change to happen. Whenever one of my clients becomes aware of something new, they almost always ask some version of the questions, "How do I change that?" or "What do I do now?" I encourage them to simply grow in awareness and allow change to flow naturally from that awakened place inside.

Living It Out 🌿 How could you grow deeper in awareness—by journaling, talking with a friend, praying, going for a walk, reading a book, listening to a podcast? Reflect on what would help you grow in awareness this week.

Day 4 Prompt: Defying Shame

What I didn't mention about my coffee shop conversation is that my friend was also navigating her own waiting season. She was able to empathize because she also knew what it was to be angry with God.

If we agree with the lie that we are alone in our pain, we slip into the trap of self-pity. Courage to open up about our struggles can create powerful connection. The timing of this devotional is special because while writing it, my friend's waiting came to a close as she shared news of her pregnancy.

When we allow each other into the waiting, we can celebrate together in a profound way when the season changes.

Living It Out 🌿 How can you be brave in your community this week? How can you celebrate the end of a friend's season of waiting while still in your own? Write down what this act of bravery could be for you and what it means to acknowledge both the celebration and perhaps sadness of celebrating a friend.

You do not realize
now what I am doing,
but you will [fully]
understand it later.

John 13:7, AMP

Faith and Control

Like the wind You'll guide
Clear the skies before me
And I'll glide this open sea.[1]

"CAPTAIN" BY BENJAMIN HASTINGS AND SETH SIMMONS

YEARS AGO I HEARD AN ANALOGY about a ship and a train, which I never forgot.

A preacher was talking about faith and illustrated his thoughts by contrasting travel on a ship and a train. When you're on a train, he said, the feeling underneath your feet is predictable and reassuring. You can feel yourself moving forward in the intended direction.

When you're on a boat, however, the feeling underneath your feet is unsteady and unpredictable. Before modern technology, a ship captain charted his path by the stars, and a conductor moved his train forward on sturdy tracks. On a train, there is no room for guessing; the path is clear and the destination nearly guaranteed.

Waiting, and the faith it requires, is more like traveling by boat. Lack of control over the when, where, how, and what of our lives can make us feel anxious and insecure. We strategize about how to remedy our situation and ruminate on how much easier it would be if we could predict outcomes and control the timing.

This faith is an invitation to board a ship and trust God to chart our paths. What if the destination is just as secure as traveling by train and the captain just as capable as a train's conductor, but the feeling underneath our feet is just *really* different? This means we need to learn how to find security from an internal place not rooted in external conditions.

The psychology term *locus of control* refers to the degree that someone believes outcomes result from their own choices and behaviors (internal locus) or from forces outside themselves (external locus).

What we believe about the agency we have or don't have determines much about our overall well-being. Research shows that those with an external locus of control "blame outside forces for their circumstances, don't believe that they can change their situation through their own efforts, and feel hopeless or powerless in the face of difficult situations." On the other hand, those with an internal locus of control are "more likely to take responsibility for their actions, have a strong sense of self-efficacy, and feel confident in the face of challenges."[2]

It's as important to grow in trusting ourselves as it is to grow in trusting God. If we don't trust ourselves and lack confidence to navigate difficulties, we will develop a fatalistic view where we believe outside forces (i.e., God) have all the authority and we have none. Trusting ourselves and trusting God are not mutually exclusive. Growing in self-confidence needs to happen in tandem with growing in trusting God.

When you feel panicked and unsteady aboard this proverbial ship, your connection to God is one of the most powerful remedies for fear. "From the end of the earth will I cry to You, when my heart is overwhelmed *and* fainting; lead me to the rock that is higher than I [yes, a rock that is too high for me]" (Psalm 61:2, AMPC).

When you question whether you will make it to shore, God will come alongside you as captain and friend to renew your confidence and give you strength to keep trusting.

•——— Day 1 Prompt: Living Empowered While We Wait ———•

Our waiting experiences don't exist in a vacuum. How we respond now is directly related to our previous life experiences. Other circumstances that felt out of our control affect how we feel now.

The past and present are deeply connected, which is why waiting is so triggering. Difficulty drums up lies from the past about being powerless to change your circumstances. Agreeing with these lies only reinforces an external locus of control.

As we loosen our control on externals and direct our energies inward, we grow in serenity. Although we have limited control over the external, we do have authority over what we believe and how we respond.

Living It Out 🌿 Healing can happen when we lean into triggering moments with compassion and curiosity—when we become observers, not judges, of our lives. How does this new approach change the "feeling underneath your feet" today?

Day 2 Prompt: Is God Sleeping?

One day Jesus said to his disciples, "Let's get in a boat and go across to the other side of the lake." So they set sail, and soon Jesus fell asleep. But a fierce wind arose and became a violent squall that threatened to swamp their boat. Alarmed, the disciples woke Jesus up and said, "Master, Master, we're sinking! Don't you care that we're going to drown?"

With great authority Jesus rebuked the howling wind and surging waves, and instantly they became calm. Then Jesus said to them, "Why are you fearful? Have you lost your faith *in me?*"

Shocked, they said with amazement to one another, "Who is this man who has authority over winds and waves that they obey him?"

LUKE 8:22-25

Living It Out 🌿 If you feel tossed by waves of fear and doubt, does it seem like God is asleep, neglectful of your pain and confusion? What did the disciples learn about God that you could apply to your own ship-like experience?

Day 3 Prompt: The Power of Affirmations

Moving from an external locus of control to an internal one can bring a spike in anxiety, so it's important to have tools to manage it.

Affirmations are powerful tools to reduce anxiety and reinforce a more accurate story about yourself and God. Scripture is full of affirmations that bolster you with a new narrative.

Living It Out 🌿 As you acknowledge each trigger with compassion and curiosity, write down new narratives you will speak over yourself. Here are a few to get started:

> *I am not forgotten or abandoned by God; I am remembered and deeply loved.*
> *I am worthy of love and belonging.*
> *I am fully accepted and cared for by God.*

Day 4 Prompt: Connecting with Fellow Passengers

Waiting can feel lonely, and we forget to look around and see how many others are aboard this proverbial ship with us. Since waiting is personal, we assume that no one else could understand what we're going through. Although our waiting stories are unique, the feelings we experience while we wait are similar.

Living It Out 🌿 Take inventory of those who are on this ship with you, whether through their stories or their physical presence. As you write down their names, notice your courage rise as you realize you aren't alone. "Therefore, since we are surrounded by such a huge crowd of witnesses to the life of faith, let us strip off every weight that slows us down, especially the sin that so easily trips us up. And let us run with endurance the race God has set before us" (Hebrews 12:1, NLT).

God Cares about the Details

Trust: In these wild and new unknowns,
your story is still taking shape.
MORGAN HARPER NICHOLS

ONE OF THE FEARS WE FACE while waiting is the fear of the unknown.

I remember a conversation with my therapist about this. My inquisitive nature was reeling because I was full of questions with no good answers, leading me to all kinds of assumptions about my future.

My therapist listened; then she told me a story about when her beloved dog got very sick. I couldn't imagine how this story could relate, but since my therapist has an uncanny way of sharing personal stories that perfectly connect with me, I listened carefully.

She and her husband took their sick dog to the nearest animal hospital (one they had never been to before), only to hear there was an abnormally long wait. She called another animal hospital farther away and thought the receptionist said there was a thirty-minute wait. When they arrived, they learned it was actually a *three-hour wait*. At this point, they had no choice but to wait. After a couple of hours, their dog was finally seen and ultimately kept overnight for his dire condition.

After the debacle, her friend commented that even though the situation was stressful, she was relieved they went to the second hospital: The vet who treated her dog was the best in the area, and the original hospital had a terrible reputation. My therapist checked their reviews, and sure enough, the comments were alarmingly accurate and validated her friend's claims.

My therapist used this story to gently remind me how much I don't know about my circumstances. No matter how a situation looks and feels like the worst-case scenario, unexpected gifts of protection and provision may be veiled within details I can't see at the time.

We're all tempted to believe we know everything about our circumstances. We base our confidence on what we see and hear and make assumptions that fall drastically short of the full picture. In these fall seasons of waiting, we humbly learn to remember that things we don't understand now will make sense later.

When Jesus announced he would wash his disciples' feet, Peter was appalled at the thought of Jesus lowering himself to do such a thing. Jesus responded, "You do not realize now what I am doing, but you will [fully] understand it later" (John 13:7, AMP). Peter didn't realize then that Jesus was setting the example of a servant and charging the disciples to repeat the pattern.

The context is different, but the principle is the same: As you're waiting for answered prayers, open doors, and fulfilled promises, you may not know what God is doing presently, *but you will later*. God will help you understand how he has been taking care of you—ways unfathomable to you now. I believe God cares about the details of our lives, and although nothing may make sense to you at this moment, your waiting is not in vain. Someday you will see how true God's care is for you.

•——— Day 1 Prompt: Challenging Your Assumptions ———•

When our strengths overfunction they evolve into our weaknesses. For example, I'm grateful for my strength of intuition, which helps me as a therapist. However, when I overly rely on this strength, my intuition can evolve into assumption. If I assume I understand what a client is communicating, I may miss something important in their story and a moment for my client to feel understood.

At times my intuitive nature has been in overdrive, evaluating everything and making assumptions along the way. Maybe you can relate. Sometimes we don't realize we're assuming until the Holy Spirit shows us we've read into something without relying on his guidance.

Living It Out 🌿 What assumptions have you made lately? Write them down. Then ask the Holy Spirit to show you what is actually true.

•——— Day 2 Prompt: Living by Faith, Not Appearances ———•

An excerpt from *Streams in the Desert* reminds me of this week's devotional:

> Many times [God's] execution will seem so contradictory to the plan He gave. He will seem to work against Himself. Simply listen, obey and trust God even when it seems highest folly so to do. He will in the end make "all things work together," but so many times in the first appearance of the outworking of His plans, "In His own world He is content to play a losing game."[1]

There are times when God seems to contradict himself. But here's the truth: God doesn't care about appearances, but he does care about the details. This is deeply challenging since we are very invested in appearances and determine what is possible based on them. The Kingdom of God runs on faith not sight. "For we walk by faith, not by appearance" (2 Corinthians 5:7, DLNT).

Living It Out 🌿 What are some ways God seems to contradict himself in your waiting? What does your faith show you that appearances cannot? Write down what comes to mind.

•——— Day 3 Prompt: What to Do When Facing Uncertainty ———•

For many of us, uncertainty is intolerable, and we have many strategies to prevent it or resolve it quickly.

A skill I teach clients is how to develop more tolerance for uncertainty. Instead of reverting to avoidance or problem-solving, I create a safe space to *face it and feel it* when it comes. The alternative is that we live in fear of what we refuse to acknowledge. When we face and feel uncertainty and survive the moment, we break free from the fear that tries to control us.

Thankfully, we aren't doing this facing alone. Psalm 139:12 says, "Even the darkness is not dark to you; the night is bright as the day, for darkness is as light with you" (ESV). God has authority over the dark places in your life and invites you into the light with him.

Living It Out 🌿 How have you been coping with uncertainty? Allow yourself to acknowledge the uncertainty you feel and to sit with it. Journal what that's like for you.

—————— **Day 4 Prompt: Phone a Friend** ——————

When my therapist's friend brought clarity to her stressful ordeal, everything changed for her. If my therapist hadn't talked with her friend, she may not have learned how well she was being protected and cared for.

Living It Out 🌿 Think about who you trust to speak into your situation with wisdom and clarity. Text or call and share with them about situations that have brought fear and uncertainty for you. Open your heart to receive a perspective that may bring the light and clarity you need.

The Relationship between Waiting and Worship

Waiting here for you, Lord
With our hands lifted high in praise.
"WAITING HERE FOR YOU"[1]

YOU KNOW THE PART IN A MOVIE where the main character is narrating a scene while all the other characters are frozen in time? I had a similar experience recently. I was standing in a worship service when everything and everyone around me seemed to stand still. As I looked around, I thought how interesting it is that one way we worship is by raising our hands. It dawned on me how difficult it feels to lift our hands when our hearts are heavy—as if the heaviness of our hearts makes our hands as heavy as lead.

Waiting has made my heart heavier than I can bear sometimes. Proverbs 13:12 says, "Hope deferred makes the heart sick" (NKJV). It's this heartsick feeling that makes our hope tired and our hands heavy.

I recently read an article titled "The Psychology of Waiting: 8 Factors that Make the Wait Seem Longer"; it outlines the experiences of consumers in retail stores, hotels, amusement parks, and hospitals. One of the many ideas discussed is how "unoccupied time feels longer than occupied time."[2] This is why a place like Disney inundates you with entertainment as you wait for hours in one-hundred-degree weather for the thrill of a three-minute ride. They understand that if you can focus on something else while you wait, your whole waiting experience will feel different.

There is a mysterious relationship between worship and waiting. The pain of waiting can make worship feel hard and nonsensical. When we're hurting, worship may be the last way we want to occupy our time. We're disappointed and angry, and usually with God. But when we bravely choose to acknowledge our hurt, open our hearts to God, and shift our focus onto him, worship becomes an antidote to the heaviness we feel.

We aren't worshiping in spite of our pain but in full view of it. As we do, our hearts soften and we gain much-needed perspective. Suddenly we have someone to focus on, and the time spent waiting feels different.

Hebrews 12:12 says, "Be made strong even in your weakness by lifting up your tired hands *in prayer and worship.*"

In our pain, we mindfully choose to lift our hands and hearts to God. As we do, we trade some of the heaviness we've been carrying for an ease and joy in our worship. Although we may still be waiting, the choice to shift our focus has the power to transform our whole waiting experience.

Day 1 Prompt: The Many Ways We Worship

Worship takes on many forms and is not confined to church services. We worship when we pray, when we journal, when we meditate, and when we share in a community.

What difficult aspect of waiting is currently affecting your worship? Perhaps shame is impacting your ability to share honestly in your community. Or maybe praying seems hard because you feel that God is absent in your life.

Living It Out 🌿 Allow God to meet you where you are. Acknowledge your hurt, and bravely choose to do the very thing you don't want to do. My guess is that whatever form of worship feels most difficult is exactly the one you need the most to relieve your heart of pain.

Day 2 Prompt: Inviting God into Our Worship

Now that you know what kind of worship has been most difficult for you recently, slow down and intentionally invite God into it. If it's journaling, write God a letter expressing your pain and questions about your waiting. If it's musical worship, put on a favorite worship song. Close your eyes and open your heart to allow the Holy Spirit to meet you in this moment.

Living It Out ❧ If your difficult area of worship is prayer or meditation, try this simple exercise: Close your eyes and breathe deeply until you feel grounded in your body. Imagine yourself in a safe place, a familiar place, or somewhere you have never been. Invite God to be here with you. Share with him what is on your heart. Notice how he responds. What does he say? What gestures of love does he offer? When you're ready, take a couple of deep breaths and open your eyes.

——— Day 3 Prompt: Participation over Passivity ———

God wants our participation, not our passivity. When our hearts feel like a ton of bricks, we assume it's God's sole responsibility to relieve us of the heaviness (especially if we blame him for it).

A number of my favorite stories in the Bible have one commonality: participation with God. Consider Joshua approaching the Jordan River with the children of Israel after waiting forty years in the wilderness. God instructs Joshua to tell the priests carrying the Ark of the Covenant to go and stand in the river. As soon as the priests set foot in the Jordan, the water flowing downstream is cut off so the children of Israel can pass on dry ground (Joshua 3:7, 14-17).

God's plans involve the participation of his people. I know how discouraging waiting is, and I know it feels like nothing you do matters, *but it does.* Worship is one way you can participate with God. When you worship, you are locking arms with God while you wait. It is one of the most powerful displays of your faith in God, and it's your faith that moves the most obstinate situations in your life.

Living It Out ❧ Read Matthew 18:18-20 and reflect on what participation with God looks like in this season.

Day 4 Prompt: The Effect of Worship on Our Brains

According to an article by Dr. Caroline Leaf, a study conducted on Carmelite and Franciscan nuns showed positive changes in their brains when they engaged in worship. What stood out to me most was the finding that "as people sing together in worship to God, as in a choir for instance, their heartbeats actually synchronize. In other words their hearts beat as one."[3]

Living It Out 🌿 If you have been feeling lonely, I hope you find this information on the power of communal worship encouraging. How can moments of communal worship help to infuse your mind, heart, and body with courage and resolve? Write down what comes to mind.

When God's Face Is Covered

Now we see but a faint reflection of riddles and mysteries as though reflected in a mirror, but one day we will see face-to-face.

I CORINTHIANS 13:12

IF YOU HAVE PLAYED PEEKABOO WITH A BABY, then you know how adorable it is to watch her puzzled expression when your face is half-covered, then see her ecstatic reaction when you reveal your face and squeal "Peekaboo!" Psychology offers an interesting explanation for this phenomenon.

According to Jean Piaget, a Swiss psychologist, *object permanence* is the understanding that objects continue to exist even when they cannot be observed.[1] It is one of the most important accomplishments for children, as without it, objects would have no separate and permanent existence in their minds.

A baby is enamored with peekaboo because she hasn't achieved object permanence yet. When you cover your face, she believes you cease to exist. Revealing your face and announcing "Peekaboo!" is like an impressive magic trick.

This idea is reminiscent of how faith is described in the Bible. "Faith shows the reality of what we hope for; it is the evidence of things we cannot see" (Hebrews 11:1, NLT).

Faith beckons us to believe that something exists even when we cannot observe it. Waiting challenges us to put this kind of faith into practice, and as we do, we grow spiritually.

Just as a baby develops the necessary skills to believe someone exists even when she cannot see their face, we, too, are developing the faith to believe in God's promises even when so much obstructs our view.

I would call this "spiritual object permanence."

Waiting moments are an invitation from God to apply faith—*the belief in a reality we cannot observe*—to our current circumstances. God is forming in us the same quality of vision the heroes of faith had. Hebrews 11:13 says, "They *saw* beyond the horizon the fulfillment of their promises and gladly embraced it from afar."

When God's face seems covered, we choose to believe God hasn't forgotten us. When our next steps are unclear, we choose to believe God is providing what we need and teaching us how to partner with him in the process. When we've waited so long our hearts ache more with every passing day, we choose to allow God to comfort us as we bravely anticipate the good awaiting us.

— Day 1 Prompt: Shifting Our Focus —

We hear the word *narcissism* a lot these days, and although it is misappropriated at times, it still speaks to a real human experience. In brief, narcissism is an inflated sense of self-importance that leads to a variety of challenges, especially in relationships. At the core of narcissism is deep-seated insecurity and a stunted ability to see beyond oneself.

It's likely that individuals struggling with narcissism didn't receive the necessary love in childhood to develop a strong sense of self. As a result, they overcompensate to divert *from* and make up *for* the insecurity they feel.

Whether or not we identify with narcissism, it's easy to become self-focused. It's important that we allow the maturation process in our lives, both mentally and spiritually. This process develops our capacity to believe that realities can exist outside of ourselves. The discomfort of waiting is one of the most powerful means to mature us from one stage of spiritual development to the next.

Living It Out 🌿 Journal how your waiting experiences have challenged you recently to grow from one stage of spiritual development to the next.

Day 2 Prompt: God Is Training Us

As we grow in spiritual object permanence, God engages us as any good parent would. He encourages us when we're afraid and teaches us how to bear uncertainty.

> In this hope we were saved [by faith]. But hope [the object of] which
> is seen is not hope. For who hopes for what he already sees?
> ROMANS 8:24, AMP

God is training us in hope—to expect good even though we can't see it. God is training us in faith—to believe there is evidence to substantiate our hope. God is training us in love—to receive and give affection unconditionally.

> Now there remain: faith [abiding trust in God and His promises],
> hope [confident expectation of eternal salvation], love [unselfish
> love for others growing out of God's love for me], these three
> [the choicest graces]; but the greatest of these is love.
> I CORINTHIANS 13:13, AMP

Living It Out 🌿 Ask God how he is using your waiting experiences to train you in faith, hope, and love—and for what purpose. Journal what comes to mind.

Day 3 Prompt: Reinterpreting God's Delays

My devotional books are tattered and well-loved. One of my favorites is *Streams in the Desert*, by L. B. Cowman. She quotes Charles Spurgeon, who says this about the moments when God's face feels hidden:

> And oh! above all, when thy God hides His face, say not that He
> hath forgotten thee. He is but tarrying a little while to make thee
> love Him better; and when He cometh, thou shalt have joy in the
> Lord, and shalt rejoice with joy unspeakable. Waiting exercises our

grace; waiting tries our faith; therefore, wait on in hope; for though the promise tarry, it can never come too late.[2]

Spurgeon encourages us to be mindful about how we interpret moments when we feel forgotten by God. He invites us to consider how the delay speaks more to God's remembrance than it could ever speak to his forgetfulness.

Living It Out 🌿 Write down how you have been interpreting God's delays and how you could reinterpret them to see all the ways he is remembering you.

Day 4 Prompt: How We Show Up Matters

How we choose to show up in the world matters. As we grow in our ability to believe prayers are being answered, promises are being fulfilled, and God is being faithful, we impact those around us in ways we may never realize.

> Wrap your heart tightly around the hope that lives within us, knowing that God always keeps his promises! Discover creative ways to encourage others and to motivate them toward acts of compassion, doing beautiful works as expressions of love.
> HEBREWS 10:23-24

Living It Out 🌿 Reflect on the areas God has been developing in you. Write down how this process is impacting the way you show up in the world.

Seeing Through

The Lord looks over us from where he rules in heaven.
Gazing into every heart from his lofty dwelling place.

PSALM 33:15

I MET MY CLIENT FOR OUR SESSION and immediately noticed how nervous they were. Between darting eye contact and uneasy body language, I could feel anxiety radiating through the room. When we sat down, I asked how they were doing.

With a wide-eyed look, they squeaked out, "Good!" while wringing their hands and looking at everything but me.

Kindly I asked, "Are you feeling overwhelmed?"

That brought a nervous laugh. "Oh my gosh, how do you know that? Ughh, it's so weird that you can tell just by being with me for like one minute!"

I suggested starting with a guided meditation, and eventually my client became visibly more relaxed.

What was unnerving to my client that day was not so much that I saw them, but that I saw *through* to their felt pain. Although it brought discomfort at first, after a few deep breaths, they were able to relax into it.

It is powerful to be seen, and in some ways, even more powerful to be seen *through*. In pain and loneliness, we often feel torn between the desire and the fear of being seen. Being seen through our pretense highlights this internal conflict.

In John 8:12, Jesus refers to himself as "the light of the world. Whoever follows [him] will not walk in darkness, but will have the light of life" (ESV). And in Matthew 5:14, 16, Jesus attributes this same light to us when he says, "You are the light of the world. . . . Let your light shine before others" (ESV).

Consider the way light shines through the stained-glass windows in an old church and illuminates the inside with beautiful rays of color. In the same way, God's light pierces us and sees *through*. This can feel exposing, so how safe we feel with God determines whether we will allow his light to enter the tender places in our hearts.

We are also light that illuminates dark places for each other, like with my client that day. I created a safe space to slow down, breathe, and reconnect with mind and body until they felt safe enough to be seen.

Take a few moments to reconnect with yourself and God. As fear dissipates and safety takes its place, step into God's loving light and allow yourself to be seen and seen *through* to peace and freedom.

Day 1 Prompt: Taking a Deep Breath

In Bessel van der Kolk's book *The Body Keeps the Score*, he discusses the two branches of our nervous system: the sympathetic (SNS), "the accelerator," and the parasympathetic (PNS), "the brake."[1]

Van der Kolk says that when we inhale, we activate the SNS, and a burst of adrenaline speeds up our hearts. Exhaling, in turn, activates our PNS and slows down the heart. This simple act of breathing helps relieve our bodies of stress.

My client needed to slow down and breathe before discussing their feelings. By offering ourselves the same courtesy when we feel overwhelmed, our minds and hearts will be more open to receive from God and others.

Living It Out Close your eyes and breathe slowly in through your nose to a count of four, holding at the top for a count of four, and then out through your mouth to a count of four. This is called box breathing.[2] Do this until you feel your body relax and your thoughts slow.

Day 2 Prompt: Changing Our View of God

We feel safe with others when we know they won't judge us. Many of us haven't felt safe with God because we see him more as a judge ready to execute judgment than as a loving parent postured to extend mercy. It's impossible to allow his light to shine on us if we expect him to judge what he sees. The first step is to evaluate if we have the most accurate view of God as kind, safe, and loving.

Living It Out 🌿 Read the story of the Prodigal Son in Luke 15 and pay attention to the father. Write down any differences between how you see this father and how you've seen God. Notice how safe you would feel with God if you knew he was like this father.

———————— Day 3 Prompt: God Touches to Heal ————————

As a little girl, one of my favorite movies was *Beauty and the Beast*. One key scene is when the Beast gets injured rescuing Belle from a pack of wolves. When Belle tends to his wounds, he reacts in anger, not only because the wounds hurt, but also, I'm guessing, because it feels vulnerable that she sees him this way.

This makes me think of Jesus placing mud on the blind man's eyes in John 9, or when he healed the leper in Matthew 8, or restored the man with the withered hand in Mark 3. They needed Jesus' touch to experience healing, but I wonder if the blind man winced when Jesus touched his eyes, or the leper felt afraid of being touched after so long. They risked allowing God to see and touch the painful parts of their stories.

Living It Out 🌿 What pain are you afraid to let God see and touch? Think about the statement below, and write down what comes to mind.

Jesus doesn't see to bring more shame or touch to inflict more pain; he sees to impart compassion and touches in order to heal.

———————— Day 4 Prompt: Knowing Your Values ————————

My friend Savannah and I used to host a podcast. In one episode I shared an exercise I do to help clients identify their top values.

Savannah's top value of authenticity has encouraged me to allow others to see me as I am, not only how I want to be seen. And my top value of honesty has encouraged her to be more forthcoming with her thoughts and feelings.

I want the same for you—to be real with yourself and feel confident that people want to see you as you are, even when you're uncertain.

Living It Out  To discover your top value, do an online search of the "List of Values" from Brené Brown. Write your top ten values in no particular order. Eliminate each lesser value until you reach your top one. Rewrite your list in its new order from one to ten. Consider how you can see others and allow yourself to be seen as you live into these values.

Wrap your heart tightly
around the hope that
lives within us, knowing
that God always keeps
his promises!

Hebrews 10:23

WINTER

IN HER BOOK *Wintering: The Power of Rest and Retreat in Difficult Times*, Katherine May says this about winter: "I'm certain that the cold has healing powers that I don't yet come close to understanding. After all, you apply ice to a joint after an awkward fall. Why not do the same to a life?"[3]

The cold can be unpleasant and uncomfortable, but that doesn't mean it's not useful. We associate the helpful with the comfortable and glibly discard our winter seasons assuming they have nothing to offer. It's tempting to see winter as something to move through quickly, but there is profound wisdom that can only be gathered here—lessons of trust, rest, and faith. The unpleasant conditions of winter are what challenge us to go inward and discover what's there . . . wrestling, inquiring, and uncovering.

Waiting in winter involves less creature comforts, which challenges any superficiality and invites us to confront what we have been avoiding in other seasons. Spring brings warmth and beautiful budding blooms; summer brings vacationing and endless opportunities for fun; and fall is still warm and beautiful enough to evade the more difficult inner work that presents itself in winter.

As the canopy of winter settles over our world, we can no longer outrun the invitation to pause and reflect. Winter demands a slower pace because of conditions outside our control. Our questions, struggles, and unrefined natures lay as bare as the trees that surround us. This is when some of the deepest work takes place.

We don't naturally want to lean into winter, but its long embrace relaxes our stiff and unrelenting hearts as we learn to release control. As we settle into this season, we surrender to the deep and unglamorous work that can only be done here.

Winter carries hidden beauty. So much life is being preserved and stored away to be revealed in a later season. Although it looks dormant, it is not inactive. Words in winter breathe life into tired places and remind us that even here—especially here—there is still purpose.

Letting Yourself Be Seen

*Courage starts with showing up
and letting ourselves be seen.*
BRENÉ BROWN, *DARING GREATLY*

MY MOVE TO NASHVILLE IN 2018 was my third one in four years, and it felt bittersweet. It was tempting to put my life on hold until I had that some*thing* or some*one* I'd been waiting for. But I refused to stop living, even if it meant making this move on my own.

Five days after the move, my new friend Savannah announced that she was hosting a Bible study for women in her home. I messaged her and said I would love to join if there was space. She replied back in all caps, "BARB, YES, THERE IS ALWAYS SPACE FOR YOU." That gathering led to years of dinners and deep friendships.

One evening, I showed up to Savannah's feeling particularly sad about my season of waiting. I'm exceptionally skilled at the art of deflecting—asking questions of others to sidestep the vulnerability of talking about myself. It didn't take long before I realized this "skill" was not going to fly with this group of friends.

Savannah placed a few random household items on the table and had us choose the object that best reflected how we felt. I panicked, suspecting this exercise would bust my heart wide open.

It did. I chose a clock because it represented the pressure I felt about losing time. The longer I waited for what I wanted, the more terrified I became.

When my turn came to share, I described why I chose the clock, but I had no idea that I was using words like *we* and *you* to name my own pain.

Savannah stopped me, and with a curious boldness she said, "Try saying 'I and me' instead of 'you and we' to describe how *you're* feeling." I was hot with embarrassment because my unconscious efforts to keep distance from my painful emotions had failed.

Sharing my truth was messy, and I couldn't keep it together anymore or tie up the pain with a bow. You could hear a pin drop as I cried and fumbled for words. Tara put her hand on my arm. Jamie channeled love and strength with her laser-focused eye contact. Sarah and Savannah showed empathy through their own tears. And Catherine offered wise words of encouragement. It was so healing.

As a therapist, I call this a *corrective experience*—a moment when lies are exchanged for truth, and painful past experiences lose their power in the light of a new healing one. When my friends held my pain with safety and love, they reflected the words of Jesus in John 13:35: "Your love for one another will prove to the world that you are my disciples" (NLT).

Move past resistance about sharing your pain and vulnerability with friends, and let it happen. Allow yourself to be seen and supported by God's love through others.

• ———— Day 1 Prompt: Learning to Take Up Space ———— •

All of us have subtle ways of deflecting unwanted attention. When someone genuinely asks how we're doing, it can be hard to answer the question because we fear taking up too much emotional space. It's easier to deflect by giving a quick response and moving on.

Questions can be painful at times. It's okay to stay on the surface with an honest yet simple answer if you aren't ready to take a deep emotional dive. And it's okay to be vulnerable and take up the space you need when it feels safe.

Living It Out 🌿 How have you deflected attention from yourself, and what are you trying to protect yourself from? Write your answers as they come to mind.

Day 2 Prompt: Reshaping Our View of God

Our powerful and painful experiences shape what we believe about ourselves and the ways we show up in the world. Those experiences can lead to misguided ideas about faith, making it difficult to fully trust God.

Living It Out 🌿 What do you believe to be true about God in light of your circumstances? What do you need from God—to feel his presence, to know his concern, or to know he sees you? Write what comes to mind, and allow this awareness to clear a path for a new experience with God.

Day 3 Prompt: Choosing to Be Brave

You may have experiences that can only be explained as "God led me here." One of the biggest reasons God leads us to new places is for the people we will meet. I experienced this in my move to Nashville. Pushing through pain and loneliness is worth the effort for the new connections you gain on the other side of your bravery.

Living It Out 🌿 How have you struggled to be brave because of a painful waiting season? What kind of brave choice do you sense God asking you to make, and what do you hope God has in store for you on the other side? Listen to the song "You Make Me Brave" by Amanda Cook as you reflect on your answers to these questions.

Day 4 Prompt: Seeing God through Others

As much as this week's devotional is about finding community in a new place, it is also about experiencing God's love through community.

St. Teresa of Avila is credited with saying, "Christ has no body but yours, No hands, no feet on earth but yours, Yours are the eyes with which he looks [with] Compassion on this world, Yours are the feet with which he walks to do good, Yours are the hands, with which he blesses all the world."[1]

The pain of waiting can make our relationship with God feel complicated. When talking to God feels hard, sometimes we need to talk with those God has lovingly placed in our lives. Sitting across a table from a trusted friend or receiving a hug in silence when our words fall short are expressions of God's love. As we're comforted by others, we are also comforted by God.

Living It Out 🌿 What do you need from God in this particular moment through the people in your life—a conversation, a hug, a kind act, or something else? Write down what you need, and then be brave by sharing this need with a friend. Also, list the ways your community has already reflected God's love toward you.

When Promises Feel like Empty Tombs

Faith is the bird that feels the light and sings when the dawn is still dark.
RABINDRANATH TAGORE,
THE ENGLISH WRITINGS OF RABINDRANATH TAGORE

WAITING INCLUDES ANTICIPATION.

Anticipation is defined as "the act of looking forward"[1] and is rooted in the brain's cerebellum. When we anticipate something, our brains desire more dopamine, a chemical that stimulates arousal.[2] This heightened state can be exhausting, like constantly sitting on the edge of our seats.

When time drags on and we're tired from anticipating but never receiving, we need permission to keep believing. The 8,810 promises[3] in the Bible show how much God understands this struggle. In the uncertain space between waiting and fulfillment, we long for solid ground to stand on.

The word *promise* is defined as "a declaration that one will do or refrain from doing something specified, a reason to expect something, ground for expectation of success, improvement, or excellence."[4]

Promises steady our hearts and give us that solid ground. However, promises can feel both encouraging and discouraging. Since they speak to the unseen reality of our faith, they challenge the current reality staring us in the face.

A particular story in the Gospels illustrates this conflict well. In Luke 24, we read of a company of women arriving at the tomb early in the morning to grieve Jesus' death. They are shocked to discover the stone rolled away from the tomb's entrance. Two angels appear and remind them of Jesus' promise to rise again. As they remember these words, their depleted hearts fill with anticipation again, and they run to tell everyone they know.

The story then transitions to two dejected men walking on the road to Emmaus. Unbeknownst to them, Jesus joins their conversation and, tongue in cheek, asks why they are sad. Their response is profound.

> Certain women of our company, who arrived at the tomb early, astonished us. When they did not find His body, they came saying that they had also seen a vision of angels who said He was alive. And certain of those who were with us went to the tomb and found it just as the women had said; but Him they did not see.
>
> LUKE 24:22-24, NKJV

The empty tomb felt like a crushing disappointment because they hadn't seen Jesus. Discovering Jesus' empty tomb may seem like the most encouraging moment, but the empty tomb was the *promise,* and they needed the *person.* Sometimes the empty tomb is discouraging until we see Jesus. Finding the empty tomb felt like discovering an empty promise.

This is liberating for us. It gives us a different kind of permission—the one that says it's okay when God's promises feel discouraging. It's okay when the potential of what will be feels more like grief and a dead end.

Winter seasons of waiting can feel harsh and never-ending, so as you anticipate the fulfillment of your desires, don't be surprised if your heart gets tired. The angels say to the women at Jesus' tomb, "Remember." What looks and feels empty may signify that life and fulfillment are on the way.

Day 1 Prompt: Honoring Our Grief

We grieve when something painful happens and when something hopeful does not. The men on the road to Emmaus said to Jesus, "We had hoped that he was the one who was going to redeem Israel" (Luke 24:21, NIV).

When the women went to Jesus' tomb, they were compelled by more than Jewish custom. They were constrained by grief and love, and they acknowledged their loss by preparing spices and oil to pour out on Jesus' body.

When our disappointments give way to grief, we might plant flowers, write a letter, release balloons, or even get a tattoo with a symbol that honors our grief.

Living It Out ✿ Take time to honor your grief. Here is a suggestion to consider: In your journal, write a letter to God, to yourself (past, present, or future), or to whatever or whomever you are waiting for.

•——— Day 2 Prompt: Traveling to Your Empty Tomb ———•

Start today's prompt by finding a quiet, safe space.

Close your eyes and take slow, deep breaths in through your nose and out through your mouth. Notice the air traveling from the base of your stomach, to your chest, to the top of your head, and out through your mouth.

Imagine traveling to *your* empty tomb. It could be a physical place or an emotional place inside. As you arrive at this place, be curious. Notice and follow your emotions and thoughts. What is your empty tomb? How does it feel to you? Why is it there? What does it represent?

Invite God into this picture, and notice what he says and does. Stay there as long as you need.

Living It Out ✿ Journal and reflect on what you noticed during this meditation.

•——— Day 3 Prompt: A Verse and a Song ———•

Consider 2 Corinthians 1:20: "No matter how many promises God has made, they are 'Yes' in Christ. And so through him the 'Amen' is spoken by us to the glory of God" (NIV).

As time passes, we are more tempted to doubt God's promises. We think the passage of time has the power to change God's yes to a no. But God's yes cannot be undermined by time. God says what he means and means what he says. He isn't fickle, and when he says yes, he means it.

Living It Out 🌿 Listen to the song "Yes and Amen" by Housefires, and reflect on what shows up for you to process.

●——————— **Day 4 Prompt: Go It Together** ———————●

Whether it was the men on the road to Emmaus or the women coming to the tomb, they traveled *together*. Community is vital while we're waiting.

Irvin Yalom, a renowned psychotherapist, described the term *universality* as "being part of a group of people who have the same experiences helps people see that what they are going through is universal and that they are not alone."[5]

Waiting is a universal human experience, and it's comforting to know we are not alone in that ache. Our aches may be different, but we can still encounter God's faithfulness together.

Living It Out 🌿 Write down practical ways you can invite someone into your waiting, and find ways to support them in theirs.

Feeling Our Feelings

Hurt leads to healing
Loneliness moves us to intimacy
Sadness expresses value and honor
Gladness proves hope of the heart to be true.

CHIP DODD

A SENTIMENT I HEAR OFTEN FROM CLIENTS is how terrifying feelings can be.

We need to believe that the reward of feeling our emotions outweighs the risks. One reason we avoid stepping into a feeling is because of unanswered questions surrounding our emotions: What will happen if I feel this sadness? Will I climb under the covers and never see anyone again? Or if I feel this anger, will I start screaming at everyone all the time?

The reality is, it's more costly when we don't feel what is ours to feel. Similar to holding a ball under water, the longer we hold it down and the further we push it under water, the more explosive it is when we remove our hands. Avoiding our emotions doesn't mean they go away. They remain inside our hearts, minds, and bodies, *waiting* to be recognized.

We know life continues to happen even when we're waiting. As many details vie for our attention, we convince ourselves it's more responsible to put our feelings on layaway. But avoidance turns our inner world into a pressure cooker. Sadness, disappointment, loneliness, and fear have a way of showing up at the most inopportune times.

I'll be absorbed in a session with a client when an emotion hits me seemingly out of nowhere. I make a mental note and add it to the growing pile to sift through later. If I don't circle back to the backlog of emotion collecting inside of me, I end up feeling stuck.

Waiting drums up many feelings, and if we don't know how to relate to them, waiting will feel like an enemy threatening our lives and desires.

Hebrews 6:12 says, "Imitate those who through faith and patience inherit what has been promised" (NIV). If it's through faith and patience that we receive what God has promised, we will need to grow in our capacity to sit with difficult emotions.

Some schools of thought separate faith and feelings as if they were in opposition, but I couldn't disagree more. If we don't create space to acknowledge how we feel, then we construct unnecessary obstacles to believing and waiting with patience.

There is tremendous value in courageously facing your inner world with God. As you wait, you are growing in faith and patience and learning to honor your humanity by feeling what is yours to feel.

• ———— Day 1 Prompt: "Emotions Are Information" ———— •

One insight that helped me understand the value of emotions is from Marc Brackett, who says, "Emotions are information."[1] In his book *Permission to Feel: Unlocking the Power of Emotions to Help Our Kids, Ourselves, and Our Society Thrive*, he explains that the more specific language we use to name our emotions, the more equipped we are to decode the information.

When I talk with clients about this, I use an analogy (not original to me) about a car dashboard, which gives us essential information about what is happening on a deeper level with the car. For example, a fuel light indicates we need to get to a gas station.

Our emotions show up like dashboard indicators—they carry vital information about what we need. Waiting brings delays, disappointments, and frustrated plans, which cue a cacophony of emotions. If we dismiss them, we heap more difficulty onto an already challenging situation.

Living It Out ꙮ What emotions are lighting up on your proverbial dashboard? How can you create space to acknowledge the information they are carrying about what you need?

•——————— Day 2 Prompt: Embracing Our Emotions ———————•

It's common to find ourselves in a negative loop regarding our emotions. The loop starts when we agree with the misguided idea that we will fall apart if we feel our emotions. If we push down our feelings, eventually they explode in a disruptive experience.

This disruption reinforces the harmful lie that emotions are threatening. The way out of this loop is to develop the skill to sit with uncomfortable feelings.

I can't find one time in the Gospels when Jesus rebuked someone for feeling emotion. I see him coming alongside people to feel what they felt (Matthew 14:14, John 11:33-38).

Living It Out 🌿 Give yourself permission to feel one emotion today, and invite God into it. Maybe it's sadness, disappointment, or anger. God is not threatened by your emotions and wants to show you how to honor them as he does.

•——————— Day 3 Prompt: Feeling and Containing ———————•

After a client and I have talked about feeling emotions, the question that follows is, "Okay, but how? How do I feel these emotions without them taking over my life?"

I explain that it's by feeling *and* containing them, similar to a seesaw. Equal weight and emphasis on feeling our emotions and containing them gives us internal balance.

When you're met with the pain of waiting and feel a rush of emotion, allow yourself time to register these emotions and what they may be communicating about your needs. After you have made space for them, contain them through a mindfulness exercise.

Living It Out 🌿 Here's one to get you started: Close your eyes and imagine any container that can hold these emotions and place them inside. Then, imagine bringing the container to a safe place. When you are ready, imagine walking away and take a few deep breaths to acknowledge what you've done.

Notice what feels different and record these differences in your journal. There are no right or wrong answers when it comes to noticing our emotions.

———— Day 4 Prompt: Faith *and* Emotion ————

Faith and emotions are designed to work in harmony. In an article about the relationship between the two, the author put it this way:

> God gives us many ways of making sense of the world around us: the Bible, tradition, friends, experience, reason, and emotion. None of these faculties are completely sufficient on their own. We can misinterpret the Bible. The church's tradition did not always get things right. Friends can misguide us. Experiences are open to multiple interpretations. Reason has its limits. Emotions do not always make perfect sense. God gives us all of these faculties to work together. Relying on just one of them can lead to a skewed view of God and the world.[2]

Living It Out 🌿 Emotions are imperfect gifts of tremendous value when we know how to relate to them. Share your thoughts about faith and emotions with a friend, and ask them what they think.

The Importance of Connection

The gift of presence is a rare and beautiful gift.
To come—unguarded, undistracted—and be fully present,
fully engaged with whoever we are with at that moment.

STASI ELDREDGE, *CAPTIVATING*

FEAR HAS A WAY OF SNEAKING UP ON US and gripping our hearts, leaving us dizzy and blindsided.

I had one of those dizzying moments recently as I was drinking my morning coffee on my porch. Within minutes, I went from feeling a twinge of sadness to drowning in despair. I let my thoughts stray down the path of doubt and disappointment a little too long, and before I knew it, I was staring up from a dark hole, wondering how I got there.

These dark-hole moments remind me of an animated video narrated by Brené Brown about the difference between empathy and sympathy. In the video, there is an empathic bear, a hurting fox, and a sympathetic deer. The video illustrates a downcast fox sitting at the bottom of a black hole, saying, "I'm stuck, it's dark, and I'm overwhelmed."

To which the bear responds by climbing down the ladder and saying, "I know what it's like down here, and you're not alone."

This empathetic response is contrasted with the deer sticking its head into the hole and asking if the fox wants a sandwich. The deer offers a string of "at least" statements in a frustrating attempt to "silver line" the fox's pain.

It's profound when Brené says, "Rarely can a response make something better. What makes something better is connection."[1]

If you have been waiting awhile, you know that insightful responses aren't always enough to ease the pain. You need comfort and hope, but even those who love you might be unsure how to offer them. This is a really difficult place to be in, especially if you're anxiously searching for answers that are nowhere to be found.

During our hardest moments, we don't need more answers; we need connection to God, ourselves, and others. We need a warm embrace from a friend or family member, and even though they may not have the answers, they have offered us the gift of their presence.

When it comes to connection with God, these two verses come to mind:

We do not have a high priest who is unable to empathize with our weaknesses.
HEBREWS 4:15, NIV

He lifted me out of the pit of despair, out of the mud and the mire. He set my feet on solid ground and steadied me as I walked along.
PSALM 40:2, NLT

In these winter seasons of waiting, God not only climbs down into our sadness with us but also lifts us out of despair and sets our feet back on solid ground. Perhaps today your waiting feels heavy, and you're looking up from a black hole. It's okay. You're not out of reach. Just as Jesus mourned with Mary and Martha over their brother, Lazarus, before he did anything miraculous, Jesus will mourn with you before he brings you out of the pit and onto solid ground again.

Day 1 Prompt: The Difference between Empathy and Sympathy

When the ache of waiting feels unbearable and a well-meaning friend or family member offers a sympathetic response like "Everything happens for a reason" or "At least it wasn't worse," you know how short it falls in comforting your heart. Sympathy feels *for* others and stands outside the hurting person's pain, which can leave him or her feeling alone. Empathy, on the other hand, is the ability to feel *with* others. It's when a person steps into our pain and says, "I'm in this with you."

Living It Out 🌿 Reflect on a time when someone sympathized with you, and recall how you felt. Contrast this experience with how you felt when someone empathized with you. Journal the differences you notice.

•————— Day 2 Prompt: The Gift of Remembrance —————•

Start today's reflections by watching the narrated video by Brené Brown and meditating on Psalm 40:2: "He lifted me out of the pit of despair, out of the mud and the mire. He set my feet on solid ground and steadied me as I walked along" (NLT).

When we're preoccupied with our circumstances changing, we lose sight of the moments when God met us in despair and encouraged us to continue believing.

Living It Out 🌿 Recall moments when God has done this for you. *Remember* the ways he has *remembered* you in your waiting, and write down each memory that comes to mind.

•————— Day 3 Prompt: The Power of Visualizations —————•

I look for every opportunity to guide a client through visualization exercises. According to an article by A. J. Adams, "a study looking at brain patterns in weightlifters found that the patterns activated when a weightlifter lifted hundreds of pounds were similarly activated when they only imagined lifting. . . . Brain studies now reveal that thoughts produce the same mental instructions as actions."[2]

Our brains are powerful, and what we visualize, we experience.

Living It Out 🌿 With this in mind, close your eyes and imagine this black hole you may find yourself in. Take a few deep breaths; then connect with what it feels like to be there. Maybe you feel sad, disappointed, and hopeless.

Imagine God climbing down into this pit with you. Notice what it feels like for him to be present in this place, and how it transforms your feelings about your present and future. Write down what you noticed.

———— **Day 4 Prompt: Connection over Responses** ————

It's tempting to try and fix pain rather than being present with it. It requires courage and vulnerability to sit with pain, which is why a response isn't always needed to make something better.

When Jesus came to Lazarus's tomb after his death (John 11), before he did anything miraculous, he *empathized.* He wept and mourned the loss of his friend, the loss of Mary and Martha's brother. Jesus could have bypassed their pain and gone straight to the miracle of resurrection, but he understood the importance of being present to others' pain.

Living It Out 🌿 Next time you're tempted to bypass pain by trying to "fix it," ask yourself if that is what's really needed. Challenge yourself to sit with the pain. As you do, journal what makes this challenging and how it feels different.

He lifted me out
of the pit of despair,
out of the mud and
the mire. He set my
feet on solid ground
and steadied me as
I walked along.

Psalm 40:2, NLT

When You Feel Left Behind

"Hope" is the thing with feathers
That perches in the soul
And sings the tune without the words
And never stops at all.

EMILY DICKINSON, "'HOPE' IS THE THING WITH FEATHERS"

A WHILE BACK, a friend and I were exchanging stories about times our futures felt out of focus and uncertain. My friend shared that she felt left behind in life. Everyone around her seemed to be catapulting into the next season of their lives, but she felt lost and exhausted. We agreed that some of our most trying times came when we felt torn between urgency to make a decision and the desire for God's direction.

A common complaint I hear as a therapist is about feeling stuck. It's often the catalyst for clients to seek therapy. Feeling stuck is immobilizing and parallels a freeze response, one of four trauma responses (along with fight, flight, and fawn).[1] When we're stuck, we feel frozen, unable to make the next move. This response could be a result of fear triggering a trauma-like response.

Our conversation reminded me of when the Israelites escaped Egypt and were traveling toward the Promised Land. They faced an impassable Red Sea and the terrifying sound of their enemies pursuing them. They froze in fear. This trauma response stemmed not only from the immediate terror, but also from four hundred and thirty years of generational trauma as slaves.

Moses offered this powerful charge: "Don't be afraid. Just stand still and watch the LORD rescue you today. The Egyptians you see today will never be seen again" (Exodus 14:13, NLT).

This story holds so much wisdom for us. If fear caused them to freeze, then faith could empower them to stand still. Their outward position wouldn't change, but their mental and emotional posture could shift from fear to faith. I'm not suggesting you need more faith to overcome fear, but exercising the faith you do have, however small, empowers you with truth that supersedes the fear of the moment.

This story also shines a spotlight on the collision between the spiritual and the natural as you make decisions. The "standing still," "not yets," and "hold ons" allow space for God to arrange circumstances so the scene and season you are walking into is prepared for you.

There are practical implications for your waiting, and God asks you to stand still so you can move forward. If you're waiting for financial provision, a healing, a breakthrough, or just the next step, God's word to you first is to stand still.

If you feel confined or lost in uncertainty, stand still and allow God to work. He is orchestrating details and guiding you into your future.

Standing still can feel like being left behind. Waiting on an invisible God can feel futile. But the posture of standing still reveals our agreement with faith over fear, and the deep belief that God can do more in our waiting than in our restless doing.

●————— Day 1 Prompt: Tracing Your Steps —————●

Imagine trying to water flowers with a garden hose that isn't working. You pull the lever, but nothing happens. In frustration, you might assume the hose is broken and throw it on the ground. Alternatively, you could compose yourself and think critically. A quick check might reveal a kink, and with a simple fix, water begins to flow.

Life isn't this straightforward and uncomplicated, but if you have been feeling stuck lately, it may have to do with a kink that has formed in your life. These kinks can include unkind words spoken to you, guilt or shame about a decision, or fear that nothing will change.

Living It Out 🌿 Take a few deep breaths and close your eyes. Envision your life as a curious observer, while you trace your steps back to check for a kink.

Write down what you notice, and ask God how to release any kinks so you can experience freedom and joy.

Day 2 Prompt: Learning to Stand Still

The Exodus story illustrates the parallel between standing still and feeling frozen.

Hearing the Egyptians coming after them caused intense fear in the Israelites. Even if there had not been a history of trauma from the Egyptians, their present circumstances were terrifying enough to cause them to freeze.

Knowing they were frozen in fear, God instructed Moses to tell the people to stand firm in faith. As we wait, we face two choices: freeze in fear or stand still in faith. They are very different positions internally. There is no shame in freezing when you're afraid. What matters is your courageous choice to respond to God's voice, no matter how weak your faith feels. When you take one step toward God, he comes running toward you.

Living It Out 🌿 What are some ways you have felt frozen in fear? What is one way you can stand still today? Take a few minutes to journal your responses.

Day 3 Prompt: Faith Helps Us See Differently

"By faith, we see the world called into existence by God's word, what we see created by what we don't see" (Hebrews 11:3, MSG). Although the context of this verse is slightly different from how I'm using it here, it helps us recognize the collision between the natural and spiritual when the Israelites escaped Egypt. The Egyptian army and the Red Sea were natural forces they could see, but they were subservient to a spiritual force they couldn't see—God's power to protect and deliver them.

Waiting can trigger fear and lead to moments when it feels impossible to accurately interpret what's happening. It's no wonder this verse begins with "By faith." It takes faith to believe there's a relationship between what we can and can't see. It takes faith to believe God hasn't forgotten us and that participating with him matters.

Living It Out 🌿 Write down an experience in your waiting story that illustrates this intersection between the natural and spiritual.

●——————— **Day 4 Prompt: Vulnerability Is Contagious** ———————●

My friend and I wouldn't have discovered similar feelings about our lives had we not courageously shared our hearts.

It's easy to assume we are alone in our struggles. One reason for this false idea is that people avoid sharing vulnerably. Consider social media: It's a highlight reel, and often scrolling leads to our thinking that everyone else's lives are perfect while our own lives are lacking.

Vulnerability is contagious, and when we pull back the curtain even a little to those we trust, we will feel less alone, and we'll inspire courage in others to share vulnerably too.

Living It Out 🌿 Who would you trust to invite behind the curtain today—a friend, family member, therapist, mentor? Write down a name, and reach out to them to share what has been on your heart.

What to Do When It's the Scariest

You know every step I will take before my journey even begins.
You've gone into my future to prepare the way, and in kindness you
follow behind me to spare me from the harm of my past.

PSALM 139:4-5

"IT'S THE SCARIEST RIGHT NOW."

I remember walking into my therapy session fearful and tired of the waiting season I was in. When I explained the pressure cooker of emotions percolating inside my heart, my therapist suggested EMDR.

EMDR, eye movement desensitization and reprocessing, is a technique used when clients feel stuck because of unresolved pain. Like my therapist, I also get excited to use EMDR with clients because I see the possibilities for healing that are hidden within the present pain.

Dr. Francine Shapiro developed EMDR in 1987 as a therapeutic technique for reprocessing traumatic events. As we move through life, we unconsciously internalize limiting thoughts, feelings, and beliefs. Since the emotional charge attached to these parts of our stories is so intense, we push them to the recesses of our minds and bodies.[1]

Back in the session, I closed my eyes as we started EMDR. My therapist asked me to be curious and follow wherever the fear I was feeling took me. I went to a memory from when I was five. My parents and I were visiting family, and as I played outside by myself, a bunny caught my eye. I chased it a half mile before realizing I was utterly lost. Panicked, I wandered around in tears. Eventually a neighbor found me and returned me to my family, who were just as panicked looking for me.

I was amazed that this memory surfaced. I hadn't thought of it in years, yet it mirrored my current feelings thirty years later. As both a five-year-old and a thirty-five-year-old, I was scared that I wouldn't find my way home, and if I did, the things I wanted and the people I loved would be gone. As my waiting dragged on, it felt like the walls of time were closing in on me.

My therapist asked me to invite my "ideal parent" into the memory. An ideal parent is any presence who embodies the safest presence you could imagine. I closed my eyes again, and as I invited my ideal parent (who, for me, is Jesus) into this memory, he came alongside my panicked five- and thirty-five-year-old selves and kindly said, "It's the scariest right now."

His words were so comforting. In between lost and found, waiting and arriving, longing and holding, asking and receiving, *is* the scariest place.

At times we will feel lost, and we'll need God to validate how scary it is to straddle the worlds of hope and fulfillment. We need to hear him say he hasn't forgotten us and has gone ahead to provide what matters most. We need to see God as the kind neighbor who saw me wandering around, able to reunite me with my family.

I hope you sense God drawing near to find you and validate your fears. I hope you feel hope rising as you realize how committed God is to protecting and providing for you every step of the way.

•——— Day 1 Prompt: How to Write a Brave New Ending ———•

EMDR allows us to heal painful parts of our stories. Therapists use vibrating tappers that toggle from one hand to the other, or headphones that beep from one ear to the other, to produce a rhythm that encourages the brain's right and left sides to communicate. This allows you to revisit and reprocess memories safely so you can experience healing.

Imagine that your brain is like a warehouse containing files of memories, emotions, beliefs, and narratives. EMDR activates these files. Your brain activity increases, and your whole memory network is awakened—conscious and unconscious, it's all connected.

Oftentimes we don't explore these inner places for fear of what we'll find. Brené Brown says, "When we deny our stories, they define us. When we own our stories, we get to write a brave new ending."[2]

Living It Out 🌿 You can incorporate this technique on your own:

1. Reflect on a negative thought, feeling, or belief.
2. Write down what comes to mind.
3. Identify a negative belief you've been rehearsing (i.e., "I'm unworthy," "I'm not enough"); then identify the positive belief you can exchange for it (i.e., "I am worthy of love," "I am enough").
4. Sit with your eyes closed, or go for a walk and alternate tapping your legs as you speak this positive belief over yourself. Connect with the words, and repeat them until you feel a shift in your mind and body.
5. Journal and reflect on this experience.

Day 2 Prompt: God as Our Ideal Parent

The term "ideal parent" may drum up a mix of emotions since not all of us experienced healthy parental relationships growing up.

Dr. Daniel P. Brown, a psychologist who helps adults heal from attachment disturbances,[3] uncovered how this ideal parent acts as a stabilizing presence when we revisit difficult parts of our stories. This presence can be God, a friend, a mentor, a spouse, and even yourself now as a healthy adult. This ideal parent also acts as an empathetic witness and unburdens us from loneliness.

Jesus' questions in Matthew 7:9-11 help us to see God this way: "Do you know of any parent who would give his hungry child, who asked for food, a plate of rocks instead? . . . How much more ready is your heavenly Father to give wonderful gifts to those who ask him?"

Living It Out 🌿 Ask yourself,

1. What experiences make it difficult to see God as an ideal parent?
2. What do Matthew 7:9-11 and James 1:17 communicate about God as your ideal parent?
3. What characteristics make God an ideal parent for you?

Day 3 Prompt: A Letter to God

I regularly pause to give my clients space to write a letter. Letter writing is a powerful exercise that helps us process. It often feels less intimidating to write out our thoughts and feelings before trying to say them out loud.

Take time to write to God. Share with him what has come up for you: your thoughts, fears, hesitations, hopes, and expectations.

Living It Out 🌿 Allow your writing to flow freely; then read the letter out loud to God, as if he were sitting with you.

Day 4 Prompt: The Gift of Compassion

Being lost, literally or figuratively, feels disorienting. The neighbor who reunited me with my family not only witnessed what I was going through but also helped me when I was unable to help myself.

Jesus told the story of a man who had been attacked by robbers. A priest and a Levite passed by the man, but a Samaritan "came along, and when he saw the man, he felt compassion for him" (Luke 10:33, NLT). Sometimes we will be the one hurting, and other times we will be like the Good Samaritan who comes alongside someone else.

Living It Out 🌿 Reflect on those who have supported you in your darkest moments. Write down how they impacted you and how you can extend compassion toward others in their difficult moments.

Time, Slow Down

IN 2010, I LIVED IN ZAMBIA, AFRICA, where I noticed almost immediately how slowly time moved. I would sit on my bed in the stillness of the morning as I drank my coffee and listened to the birds singing in the lemon and avocado trees outside my small home.

I had left America reeling from the heartache of a broken relationship and found that Africa's unhurried pace allowed me to catch my breath and put the pieces of my heart back together. The slowness was healing for me.

Waiting became commonplace. An evening at a local restaurant took two hours before the food was even served. Taking public transportation required a few hours to get wherever you needed to go. Even a casual "hello" on the street often turned into a lengthy conversation. This newfound pace in a deeply painful season sparked my desire to better understand time from God's perspective.

I came across a fascinating Greek word, *pleroma,* which means "fullness, full measure, abundance, completion or what fills."[1] In Galatians 4:4 (ESV), which reads, "When the fullness of time had come, God sent forth his Son," the apostle Paul uses the word pleroma to illustrate a picture of contents being poured into a container to explain the particulars that determine when the "timing is right" in our lives. It's only when the container has been completely filled with these contents that the fullness of time has been achieved. This description stopped me in my tracks and captured my attention.

It's difficult to understand God's timing. We assume nothing is happening because we aren't privy to what's happening behind the scenes. People say, "God is working while you're waiting," but what does that actually mean? Understanding *pleroma* demystified the process and provided clarity for my questioning heart.

The idea of fullness reminds me of the word *integration*. Pain creates fractures in our hearts, so as we slow down, we allow the healing work of integration to happen. Waiting appears to threaten our desires, but in reality it teaches us to lean into a slower pace so God can gather these broken pieces and make us whole again.

Pleroma helps us understand that waiting is not inactive or passive. As we step into the work of wholeness, we collaborate with God in our integration and the timing of our desires. Your desires and the integrity of your life are equally valuable to God.

There is no formula for answered prayers and fulfilled desires. But God cares about our character, and he often uses waiting to heal us so we can fully enjoy what we long for. Step into the slow rhythm of waiting, and allow God to do his integrative work. Your waiting matters to him. Your desires matter to him. *You* matter to him.

Day 1 Prompt: "Let's Slow Down around That"

I often say to clients, "Let's slow down around that." They usually flash a frustrated expression because they know slowing down requires them to confront pain that feels scary.

Waiting for anything requires changing our pace. Waiting is an invitation to slow down around uncomfortable parts of our stories. In the process, our impatient natures are refined.

Living It Out 🌿 How might God be inviting you to slow down? Write down what area this may be and what you think God may want to say to you.

—————— **Day 2 Prompt: What God Takes into Account** ——————

A friend once said, "It takes God a long time to work suddenly." God relates to time very differently than we do.

Second Peter 3:8 says, "A single day counts like a thousand years to the Lord Yahweh, and a thousand years counts as one day." It's mind-boggling to consider the difference. The verse that follows provides insight into God's intention.

> Contrary to man's perspective, the Lord is not late with his promise
> to return, as some measure lateness. But rather, his "delay" simply
> reveals his loving patience toward you, because he does not want any
> to perish but all to come to repentance.
> 2 PETER 3:9

God is accounting for precious details that cannot be rushed in your life, others' lives, and the world at large. Even though it's hard to see, God is at work fulfilling promises that will have the greatest impact not only in your life but also in the lives of those around you.

Living It Out 🌿 Think of another time when it seemed like God "took a long time to work suddenly." Write what you remember, what you learned about God, and your gratitude for God's timing.

—————— **Day 3 Prompt: The Process of Becoming Whole** ——————

One intervention I use with clients is called Internal Family Systems (IFS), or "parts work." IFS helps us understand the parts of ourselves that protect us from real or perceived threats. The goal is to unburden and restore our woundedness and integrate a harmonious internal world.

When you say, "Part of me wants to do this, but another part of me wants to do that," you're recognizing how parts of yourself think and feel differently.

Waiting often intensifies the tension between these parts, which creates opportunities for healing and integration. While we're waiting for God to answer our prayers, we are partnering with him in the integration of our hurting and broken parts.

Living It Out 🌿 Which parts of yourself can you identify, and how is God making you whole in your waiting? Reflect on this and write down what you notice.

Day 4 Prompt: Passing Time Together

I'll never forget the first time I got together with one of my now-close friends. We went to a yoga class and then to brunch. We talked and talked until the restaurant closed and the employees were staring intently at us to get out. Our concept of time had changed because we were so engrossed in conversation.

Time feels painfully slow when we're waiting alone. But if we're waiting with people we enjoy and care about, time moves very differently. We won't be as preoccupied with its passing because we'll be present to the people we've been gifted with in that moment.

Living It Out 🌿 Notice how being present with your community brings relief from the frustrations that come from navigating waiting alone. Share what you notice with a trusted friend.

Waves of Grief

My deep need calls out to the deep kindness of your love.

PSALM 42:7

GRIEF SHOWS UP in the big and small, and often unexpected, moments of life.

One night after a long day at work, I went grocery shopping. As I walked to my car, I felt the heavy bags cutting off circulation in my arms. In that moment, grief seeped in and reminded me how alone I felt. Looking downward, I took a deep breath and wondered if my situation would ever change.

Grief is no respecter of circumstance. And we grieve while we wait. Grief is there when you're waiting for a baby and receive a baby-shower invitation. It's there through nagging pain while you wait for physical or emotional healing. And it's there when you come home from a hard day longing for a shoulder to cry on, only to remember you're still single.

Waiting and grieving are inextricably connected. Ian Morgan Cron, author of *The Road Back to You: An Enneagram Journey to Self-Discovery*, says it isn't a question of what to *do* with our grief, but how to *be with* it.[1] The idea of being with your grief may be difficult to digest, and if you're like me, you may prefer to task it away. But resisting our grief only leads to feeling more overwhelmed.

Mindfulness expert Dr. Lynn Rossy describes grief this way: "[Grief] knows no time or boundaries. We have little control over when it decides to come up inside us. It's like a wave that builds in the ocean and then crashes into the shore. Each expression of grief ebbs and flows in amazing synchronicity with select moments of life and seems to have an intelligence all of its own."[2]

So how can we learn to *be with* our grief, riding it like a wave when it threatens to crash over us without warning? We can either resist or ride those waves. But riding waves of grief requires courage and a different kind of self-talk.

One of the ways we resist grief is with an internal voice of judgment toward ourselves or our circumstances. What we need instead is a compassionate voice that reminds us the pain is normal. We need a voice that bolsters us with strength, determination, and hope, reminding us that we won't always grieve, that we will find our way back to shore.

When it's difficult to access this compassionate voice, we can reflect on the way Jesus speaks to us:

> I will never fail you. I will never abandon you.
> HEBREWS 13:5, NLT

> My little flock, don't be afraid. God is your Father, and your Father's great joy is to give you His kingdom.
> LUKE 12:32, VOICE

> I have told you these things, so that in me you may have peace. In this world you will have trouble. But take heart! I have overcome the world.
> JOHN 16:33, NIV

When waves of grief roll in unannounced, bravely choose to *be with* your grief, and remember the kind voice of Jesus, who gives you strength to make it to shore.

•——— Day 1 Prompt: Grief Is Customized, Not Uniform ———•

Today I went to a funeral for my dear friend's dad. It was a sweet service full of tears and laughter as loved ones recounted the man he was to them. The pastor said something that resonated deeply: "Grief is customized, not uniform."

Your grief is customized not only by what you're waiting for but also by your history and who you are.

Living It Out 🌿 Learn to hold space for this idea that grief looks different for each of us. Write down ways your grief is customized to you. Then prayerfully ask how God can partner with you to bring beauty and restoration to each unique grief. Journal what comes to mind.

•——— Day 2 Prompt: The First Step toward Change ———•

Our self-talk matters, especially when we're grieving. The way we show up in the world and with others is a direct result of the internal voice we listen to. Judgmental and hopeless narratives will lead us to respond to grief and waiting in the same way—with judgment and shame.

Living It Out 🌿 The first step in addressing negative self-talk is awareness of your current internal dialogue. Consider how different you would feel about grief if you exchanged shaming narratives for God's compassionate, hopeful voice. What would God say to you while you wait?

•——— Day 3 Prompt: A Song of Grief ———•

"My eyes are dim with grief. I call to you, LORD, every day; I spread out my hands to you" (Psalm 88:9, NIV). Psalm 88 is often regarded by scholars as the "saddest psalm" of relentless grief. [3] The psalmist quite literally cried his eyes out by exhausting the lachrymal glands, necessary to keep our eyes lubricated in order to cry.[4]

Even in grief, the psalmist pours out his heart to God and waits expectantly for him to respond. This display of trust says, even here, I'm believing you can comfort me.

Living It Out 🌿 Whether your grief is past or present, write your own psalm— poem or song—that allows you to *be with* your grief while also reaching out to God in expectation that he will show up for you.

• ———— **Day 4 Prompt: Speak Your Grief Out Loud** ————— •

One reason therapy is so helpful is because we are given space to speak our thoughts and feelings out loud to someone who cares. I watch clients start to reframe their self-talk simply by hearing themselves process internal dialogue out loud. This experience also happens outside therapy, in conversation with people from our communities.

Erin Coriell, an end-of-life care advocate and grief worker, writes, "It is almost indescribable the way grief shifts in the moment it is expressed out loud. In that brief encounter, one's grief becomes the world's grief. Although pain-staking and lonely, grief is an invisible thread that connects all of our hearts. It has the power to redefine humanity."[5]

These shifts are a vital part of processing our waiting and grieving. As we hold space for each other, we feel less alone, and our pain takes on a whole different purpose.

Living It Out ❧ Take a few moments to ask yourself these questions:

1. Which trusted friend or family member can you speak your grief out loud to this week?
2. What is one way you can hold space for someone in your life who is also waiting?

I will never fail you. I will never abandon you.

Hebrews 13:5, NLT

God as Our Empathetic Witness

*Our life is full of brokenness. . . . How can we live with that brokenness
without becoming bitter and resentful except by returning again
and again to God's faithful presence in our lives?*

HENRI NOUWEN

A THERAPIST I ADMIRE ONCE SAID, "Any time you feel alone in your pain, *that*
is trauma." This one statement completely transformed the way I work with
my clients. I realized that even though our painful moments differ in severity,
it's when we bear them alone that an experience becomes traumatic.

Alice Miller, the renowned childhood researcher and psychotherapist,
coined the term *enlightened witness*, more commonly known as an *empathetic
witness*. According to Miller, an enlightened witness is a person who expresses
love toward the sufferer during a painful time in their lives. Although the
enlightened witness may not be able to remove the painful experience, they
are a validating presence who reminds the sufferer they aren't alone and that
what they are walking through matters.[1]

She addresses the question about why some who experienced abuse as
children became perpetrators of abuse later in life and why some did not. The
distinguishing factor was an empathetic witness. Those who did not repeat
their abuse with others had an empathetic witness in their lives who recognized the injustices they suffered.[2]

The role of empathetic witness is perhaps the most powerful gift I offer my
clients. I can't turn back time and reverse the pain they experienced, but I can
create a safe space to untangle the pain their trauma left behind.

Maya Angelou said, "There is no greater agony than bearing an untold
story inside of you."[3] When our stories live in isolation, we not only feel alone

but also believe we are powerless in our pain. An empathetic witness validates the sufferer's story, easing the agony.

We often don't realize that God is the ultimate empathetic witness. However, seeing God in this light may drum up a range of conflicting thoughts and feelings. When we're waiting, our prayers revolve around pleading for God to intervene and change our circumstances. We want a fixer, not a witness.

Today, settle into the idea that God is your empathetic witness. Imagine his strong and loving presence coming close to unlock the tumult of disappointment, sadness, anger, and confusion. Hear him saying that you aren't forgotten, that he's with you, and you're not alone.

Day 1 Prompt: Releasing Shame

A number of years ago, I worked with a client who had an extensive trauma history. After months of working together, I asked what the hardest part of their story was.

They paused and, looking into the distance, said, "The shame. The shame is the hardest part of my story."

When we're longing for significant change and nothing seems to materialize, we start to hear the taunting voice of shame. This voice peddles the lie that we are to blame—that *we* are flawed, and that is why our circumstances haven't improved. It's in these moments that we most need an empathetic witness to graciously speak truth over us.

Living It Out 🌿 Identify the shame you may be carrying. Close your eyes and imagine bringing this shame to God as your empathetic witness. Notice how he comes close as a safe confidant to hear your story and relieve your heart of shame. When you're ready, write down what you noticed.

Day 2 Prompt: The Many Names of God

Did you know that God has at least one hundred names?[4] Some examples are "Comforter" (Jeremiah 8:18, NIV), "Prince of Peace" and "Wonderful Counselor" (Isaiah 9:6, NLT). Each name speaks to a unique aspect of God's character. We have access to comfort, peace, and counsel in God, because that is who God is.

These roles don't contradict one another either. When God is a Comforter, he is also a Wonderful Counselor, and when God is a Wonderful Counselor, he is also the Prince of Peace. God can be our empathetic witness while also being our deliverer and defender.

"The LORD is my rock and my fortress and my deliverer, my God, my rock, in whom I take refuge, my shield, and the horn of my salvation, my stronghold" (Psalm 18:2, ESV).

Living It Out 🌿 God isn't limited, as we are. He can be many things to us at the same time. He can bear witness to our pain while also working on our behalf to answer our prayers. Reflect on today's prompt and write down your thoughts.

•——— Day 3 Prompt: Seeing God in Difficult Moments ———•

It's likely you have experienced many difficult waiting moments. Today I would like you to remember just one. Perhaps it was a moment when you were hopeful that circumstances were improving, only to have your hopes dashed to pieces.

Imagine being back in that place, both physically and emotionally. Connect with what it was like to be you. What did you need most? What was hardest about it?

Living It Out 🌿 Invite God into this scene as your empathetic witness. Notice what it's like to experience God being there with you. Stay as long as you need, and when you're ready, write down what you noticed.

•——— Day 4 Prompt: Empathetic Witnessing ———•

One of my close friends is a litigation attorney, and they had this to say about the power of a witness in a court trial:

A witness provides more credibility to the assertion of facts than the party themselves due to the vulnerable position they find themselves in. The witness speaks objectively into the same set of facts and provides a mechanism for storytelling and narrative building in a case that the lawyers cannot. Furthermore, since the credibility of the witness is less of a target, they can bring in a level of detail that those involved in the incident can't. They fill out the picture.

Just as a court witness provides these qualities, so does our community when we are in the trial of waiting. We are too close to our own stories to see them clearly. We need someone wise and caring outside of our pain to help us.

Living It Out  Write down who in your life can be an empathetic witness to remind you what is true about you and of the hope and good that exists for you now and in the future.

Healing a Broken Spirit

He would never crush a broken heart nor disregard the weak and vulnerable.
He will make sure justice comes to those who are wronged.

ISAIAH 42:3

In 2016, I moved to Chicago to finish my counseling studies. I loved navigating a new school, community, church, and city but couldn't shake the sadness of doing it alone.

In the span of ten years, I lived on two different continents and in four different states. Every time I was on the precipice of these new places and seasons, my desire for adventure conflicted with disappointment about doing it by myself.

You may know the bittersweetness of embracing change in one area while another area remains the same. You land your dream job and are still waiting for quality friendships. You and your spouse are thriving financially but still long to hold a baby of your own. You move to a new place, but physical pain travels with you. All these experiences can leave you feeling alone.

During my first winter in Chicago, life on my own had taken its toll. I sat in my car after a long day, heat blasting and the seat warmer on high. Anger, fear, loneliness, sadness, and disappointment bubbled to the surface. I didn't know what to do, so I called my mom.

After I unleashed my jumbled thoughts and feelings, my mom calmly said, "I think you have a broken spirit."

My first reaction was defensive anger, likely to cover my hurt and the fact that she was right. She reminded me of Proverbs 18:14, which says, "The spirit of a man sustains him in sickness, but as for a broken spirit, who can bear it?" (AMP). The Passion Translation reads, "The will to live sustains you when you're sick, but depression crushes courage and leaves you unable to cope."

After the call, my body felt like an incinerator from the intense emotion I was feeling. I walked around my not-so-safe neighborhood in the freezing cold to work this emotion out of my heart and body. As I walked, the words *I think you have a broken spirit* reverberated in my mind.

That's exactly it, I thought. My spirit felt crushed from years of waiting for God to answer my prayers, and it seemed impossible to keep going. I needed God to bind up my spirit, but asking him to do this was complicated. I believed God was at fault, so it felt strange to ask the same person I believed was responsible for my pain to also take it away.

Looking back, I see there wasn't one moment when God miraculously took away my pain. Instead, he healed my spirit over time. I went to bed that night understanding what needed healing, and that was enough, even though I didn't know how it would happen.

You might have a broken spirit, too, or maybe past pain still lingers. Sometimes all we need is awareness of what hurts and confidence that God will heal it. I've found that more often he heals over time, not instantly. Let God into those hurting places, and day by day he will mend your spirit and restore your joy.

• ——— **Day 1 Prompt: Being Alone versus Feeling Lonely** ——— •

Being alone does not have to equal feeling lonely. In *The Eternal Now*, theologian Paul Tillich writes, "Our language has wisely sensed these two sides of man's being alone. It has created the word 'loneliness' to express the pain of being alone. And it has created the word 'solitude' to express the glory of being alone."[1]

Being alone is a physical state of being by yourself, whereas *loneliness* is an emotional state where you feel disconnected from yourself and others.[2] Typically we experience *loneliness* when we feel unseen or misunderstood, and we experience *being alone* when we are in solitude.

Living It Out 🌿 Have you experienced moments when being alone felt lonely? Was this loneliness a result of feeling unseen or from feeling disconnected from yourself and others? Describe the factors that have contributed to your experience of both.

──── Day 2 Prompt: Vulnerability Makes Honesty Possible ────

It can be a turning point to express how it feels to ask God to heal pain he seems responsible for. God isn't interested in our religious platitudes; he wants our raw honesty. Honesty is difficult, though, because it requires our vulnerability. And vulnerability is challenging.

Part of why our spirits can feel crushed is because we resist the vulnerability that allows honesty with God. Often when we have nothing left, we finally get honest with ourselves. The more we believe in the power of vulnerability, the more willing we are to be honest.

Living It Out ❧ What do you need to be honest about related to your waiting? What scares you about being vulnerable? Write down what comes to mind, and then go on a walk and pray or journal your prayer, asking God to help you be vulnerable so you can share your heart with him.

──── Day 3 Prompt: Partnering with God ────

God is equally interested in changing our lives in a moment as he is in changing them over time (and these two usually go hand in hand). When we encounter Jesus in worship, prayer, or a conversation with a friend, life-altering healing can happen. I also believe that God changes us over time as we give ourselves to the daily work of showing up to live our lives.

God will reveal powerful truths to you, *and* you will need to partner with him so he can fully repair what was broken. A relationship with God is an ongoing dynamic that requires both parties' participation.

Living It Out ❧ How does God want to heal you? Is it by seeing a therapist and processing through past experiences? By sensing his presence as you confide in a friend? By turning on worship music and allowing the lyrics and melodies to encourage you? Write down what you need in order to experience healing.

———— Day 4 Prompt: Recognize Your Heroes ————

Clearly the hero (other than God) in my "cold night in Chicago" story is my mom. Both she and my dad have been a faithful presence through my every waiting season. The number of times I called fed up with waiting are too many to count, and each time my mom found a way to impart something I needed to hear. No parent-child relationship is perfect, but I am incredibly thankful I could pick up the phone and be met with love.

Living It Out 🌿 What heroes do you call in your most raw moments—parents, friends, mentors, your spouse? Write down their names; then call one of them and share with honesty and openness so you can receive what you need.

Sharing the Mess

Faith includes noticing the mess, the emptiness and discomfort,
and letting it be there until some light returns.

ANNE LAMOTT, *PLAN B: FURTHER THOUGHTS ON FAITH*

I'VE NEVER BEEN MUCH OF A BAKER, but every so often I'll take the browning and neglected bananas sitting on my dining room table and make banana bread.

One evening, after I mixed all the ingredients, poured them in the pan, and popped it in the oven, I looked around and laughed at the baking crime scene in my kitchen, the flour and sugar dusted across the floor. I wondered how offensive it would be to people whose kitchens look pristine through the baking process.

Our messy process is certainly not the first thing we share with the world. We are more interested in presenting a curated finished product, minus the struggle.

When we hide our messy process, we project a false picture and end up feeling alone. And we send the message that others need to do the same, leaving them feeling alone as well. I'm not suggesting we share every messy detail, but I am advocating for vulnerability with boundaries and authenticity with wisdom. The only alternatives are shame, loneliness, and a whole lot of fear.

Waiting is a messy process, full of pain, unknowns, and disappointment. If we refuse to share our process, we end up glorifying beginnings and endings and discounting the messy middle.

In Luke 17, ten lepers come to Jesus for healing. Leprosy was a highly contagious, damning disease. Lepers were exiled from their communities, never to be touched again. Many covered themselves with bandages and baggy clothing to hide their wounds and their pain, even from a distance.

We see this in how the ten lepers yelled to Jesus from afar, "Jesus, Master, have mercy on us," (Luke 17:13, ESV). When Jesus saw them, he said, "Go and show yourselves to the priests" (Luke 17:14, ESV). Jesus' instruction to go see the priests would have seemed preposterous in that Jewish culture. If these men approached a priest with leprosy still in their bodies, they would face shame from him and their community. They could let fear dictate, or they could trust Jesus' words and embrace the messy process of walking from sickness to wholeness. They chose to trust, and "as they went, they were [miraculously] healed and made clean" (Luke 17:14, AMP).

"As they went." These men risked walking toward the priest while still suffering from leprosy, and on the way, they experienced a miraculous transformation. Their process was not only on display to everyone who witnessed it but also etched in Scripture, indefinitely on display for us too.

Sharing about our seasons of waiting feels more vulnerable when we are still in process. It's uncurated, like my kitchen or the lepers' shaky steps. But the benefits of walking out our process with courage and not shying away from opportunities to share it with others outweigh any of the costs.

Day 1 Prompt: Open Doors

Most of us are familiar with electric doors—like at a mall or convenience store—that open as you approach them. One time I sat in my car late at night, squinting to make out the store's hours on the door or to spot someone inside. I knew the doors wouldn't open by staring them down or standing a hundred feet from them. I had to walk toward them, and as expected, I nearly face-planted into them before they opened wide.

The lepers' conundrum was more serious. They journeyed toward the priest without a guarantee that their leprosy would be gone. In other words, they walked toward a door not knowing if it would open or if they would feel the shock of walking into a closed one. They embraced the process of going from where they were to where they needed to be without any assurances, aside from a word from Jesus.

Living It Out 🌿 What experience in your life feels similar to mine at the convenience store or that of the men with leprosy? What has it been like when doors opened wide and when they stayed closed? Reflect and write what comes to mind.

• ————— Day 2 Prompt: God's Kindness ————— •

In seasons of waiting, God's kindness may seem put to the test.

The lepers needed to believe in Jesus' kindness in order to follow his instructions. Kindness can be described as friendly, generous, and considerate, and what distinguishes kindness from "being nice" is *sincerity*. Kindness is rooted in sincerity and authenticity. James 1:17 describes God as the "Father of lights, who shines from the heavens with *no hidden shadow or darkness and is never subject to change*" (emphasis mine). God's kindness can be trusted because he is not fickle, inconsistent, or deceptive.

Living It Out 🌿 Has the pain of waiting been difficult to reconcile with a kind God? When have you experienced God's kindness, and how did it impact you? Reflect and write what comes to mind.

• ————— Day 3 Prompt: A Balanced Perspective ————— •

As we grow in sharing our messy process, we learn how to be vulnerable with boundaries and authentic with wisdom. These balancing counterparts safeguard the sacred details of our hearts.

I heard Brené Brown illustrate this principle by describing how we determine safety when we're at the beach. As we take small steps from the shore into the waves, we pause, look around, and conclude whether it's safe. If it is, we proceed until we arrive at the depth we're comfortable with.

Vulnerability with healthy boundaries protects us from oversharing, and authenticity within the guardrails of wisdom represents our truest selves.

Being discerning and open, circumspect and tender might feel like a tenuous balancing act, but with practice you will be equipped to share your imperfect process and offer permission for others to do the same.

Living It Out  How can you practice being vulnerable while maintaining boundaries and being authentic in the context of wisdom? How much imperfect detail are you comfortable sharing about a situation? How can you allow yourself to be seen by someone you trust? Take time to determine what this practice might look like for you.

Day 4 Prompt: Highlight Reels

Social media can help us connect and share important moments, but it can be riddled with competition and comparison. It's designed to be a highlight reel that leaves most messy moments out of the picture.

Scrolling has likely led you to a post about someone landing a dream job, buying a beautiful home, or having a baby, and it pinged your heart with sadness. It's just as important to show up in online communities with wisdom and boundaries.

Living It Out ❧ Perhaps you have used social media only as a highlight reel, leaving out messy, imperfect moments. How can you engage in social media with boundaries, wisdom, and authenticity? Reflect and write down what comes to mind. Then put your ideas into action.

Unexpected Fruitfulness

The wilderness and dry land will be joyously glad!
The desert will blossom like a rose and rejoice!

ISAIAH 35:1

A COUPLE OF YEARS AGO, I visited Dallas, Texas, for a weekend work conference. It had been a full schedule, and by Sunday all I wanted to do was stay in bed and catch up on sleep. However, for reasons unknown to me at the time, I felt a strong draw to visit a nearby church.

My friends and I jumped in an Uber, and when we arrived, we found a note on the door stating, "Due to last-minute issues in our building, we moved the service to another building across town." I was faced with making a quick decision either to return with my friends to the hotel or to follow this mysterious prompting.

I said goodbye to my friends and jumped in an Uber with two girls I didn't know, who had offered me a ride to the new location. Once at the church, I walked into a sea of strangers and found a seat toward the back. After worship, the pastor greeted the congregation and began his message by reading Isaiah 54:1: "'Sing, barren woman, you who never bore a child; burst into song, shout for joy, you who were never in labor; because more are the children of the desolate woman than of her who has a husband,' says the LORD" (NIV).

He talked about a refrain that repeats through Scripture: "The God of Abraham, the God of Isaac and the God of Jacob" (Exodus 3:6, NIV). He explained that because Israel was a patriarchal culture, it was only acceptable to list the names of men. Then he made an astonishing suggestion: "What if we substituted the names of the men for the women they were married to? If we did, it would read: 'The God of Sarah, the God of Rebekah and the God of Rachel'—all of whom were barren. This tells me that God is the God of the barren."

I was stunned. This perspective flipped my view of God on its head in the best way possible. Here were three consecutive generations of barrenness: Sarah waited twenty-five years for her promised son, Isaac. Rebekah waited twenty years before giving birth to Jacob. And Rachel waited seven years to marry Jacob and at least another seven years to give birth to her first child, Joseph. And Joseph experienced barrenness of a different form— waiting in captivity for thirteen years for the fulfillment of his dreams to come to pass.

Some of Scripture's greatest players waded through the heartache of various forms of barrenness, but their stories didn't end there. Isaiah 54:1 reminds us to sing for joy in anticipation of the fulfilling gifts God intends to give us. And Psalm 66:12 says, "You have caused men to ride over our heads; we went through fire and through water; but You brought us out to rich *fulfillment*" (NKJV).

Whether you're facing barrenness in your relationships, finances, career, or future, it may be hard to imagine this place of rich fulfillment right now, and that's okay. God is leading you through your season of barrenness to a place of rich fulfillment, not only in your circumstances but also in your heart and mind.

• —————————— Day 1 Prompt: Mutual Trust —————————— •

"Do you believe God trusts you?" I posed this question to a client and watched their eyes widen as they nervously said, "Oh gosh, I don't know; I've never thought about that"—almost as if it were outrageous to think God would trust *them*.

Whenever we emphasize knowing God to the exclusion of knowing ourselves, we set the stage for failure. Any genuine relationship consists of mutual trust where each individual knows themselves enough to show up as trustworthy in the relationship. So then, why would we think it is any different with God?

God is working in us through our seasons of waiting not only to empower us to trust him but also to strengthen our ability to discern his voice. Just like I experienced on that Sunday in Dallas, the choice to follow God's prompting makes transformative and hope-giving moments possible.

Living It Out 🌿 Do you believe God trusts you? Write down your thoughts and how this mutual trust between you and God can positively impact you.

Day 2 Prompt: Minding the Nudges

Psalm 139:2 states, "You perceive every movement of my heart and soul, and you understand my every thought before it even enters my mind."

What a superpower, huh? God knows our thoughts even before they have the chance to formulate. This truth assures us that God knows what we need and when we need it. God knows our unspoken and even unacknowledged thoughts and leads us to the people and places that will bolster our hearts with strength.

Living It Out 🌿 What thoughts have you had lately about your season of waiting? Reflect what it's like for you to consider that God sees them too. Does that knowledge bring comfort, confusion, relief? Write down what comes to mind.

Day 3 Prompt: Breaking Through

I started singing in church when I was three years old. Through my hardest times, music has been an instrument to reach my heart when nothing else could. I believe music is a language all its own, able to cross every barrier and cultural divide, powerful to unite the most unlikely people. And when we're hurting, sometimes it's the only language that makes sense.

Living It Out 🌿 Listen to "Your Nature" by Kari Jobe. Allow the language to break through any hopelessness you might be feeling today. Let it clear a path in your heart to connect with God.

Day 4 Prompt: Called Aside

We don't ever fully outgrow feeling pressure to follow the group. That was how I felt with my friends that morning in Dallas. Even though they encouraged me to follow God's prompting, I still felt the gravitational pull to do what they were doing. Many times while we're waiting, God calls us aside from the norm and asks us to take a risk with him.

In your waiting, God will show you a *different way*—a way where you can belong to others while still being your own person, taking risks that stray from the well-worn path others have taken.

Living It Out 🌿 Reflect on how God may be calling you aside. Is it being in relationship with your family while you embrace new and different perspectives on life? Is it following God to a different state or pursuing a different career? Is it staying put when those around you are doing something different?

Liminal Space

To me every hour of the light and dark is a miracle.
WALT WHITMAN, "MIRACLES"

HAVE YOU EVER NOTICED how subtly night turns into morning? Any time I wake early enough to watch the night get swallowed up by the dawn, I'm left in awe.

As the sun begins to rise, the air is crisp. I feel a rush of revival as I step outside onto ground damp with dew. My neighbor's wind chime makes sweet melodies while the birds sing to wake up the world. It's the orchestra of nature we can only witness as night turns into day.

Waiting is about straddling two worlds, similar to night transforming into morning. The transformation is subtle and barely perceptible. There is a moment when it seems the night will drag on forever. We feel ourselves drawn deeper into the darkness, and we cannot imagine that we are actually moving closer to the light.

In psychology, we call this place of transition "liminal space." The word *liminal* comes from the Latin word *limen,* meaning "threshold."[1] A liminal space is the distance between what was and what will be. It is the place full of unknowns and uncertainty. We could say liminal space *is* our place of waiting. It is also where transformation takes place.

Richard Rohr says liminal space is "where we are betwixt and between the familiar and the completely unknown. There alone is our old world left behind, while we are not yet sure of the new existence. That's a good space where genuine newness can begin. . . . This is the sacred space where the old world is able to fall apart, and a bigger world is revealed."[2]

Waiting confronts who we've been and beckons us into a more whole version of ourselves. It invites us into uncharted territory of unknowns that unearth fearful questions for which we don't have certain answers.

Psalm 112:4 says, "Light arises in the darkness for the upright; He is gracious and compassionate and righteous" (AMP). Although this liminal space of transition is full of ambiguity and uncertainty, these dark places don't intimidate God. "There is no such thing as darkness with you. The night, to you, is as bright as the day; there's no difference between the two" (Psalm 139:12).

What we need most when we're moving through uncharted territory is a guide—someone who clearly sees the road in front of us and can take us by the hand and walk us from the dark into the light.

—————— **Day 1 Prompt: Who We Are Becoming** ——————

When we're transitioning from one life experience to another, we are also between one version of ourselves and another. Waiting has as much to do with heart transformation as it does with altering our circumstances.

Waiting asks a lot of us. It asks us to trust when we're afraid, to get up after a crushing disappointment, to choose vulnerability over shame, and much more. As we answer each call, we are changing and growing.

Waiting often feels like it's taking more than it's giving. The truth is, it's taking what doesn't belong—namely, negative beliefs and false ideas about God, ourselves, and others that have confined us.

Living It Out 🌿 Reflect on and write down the ways you are growing and changing as you wait.

—————— **Day 2 Prompt: God as Our Guide** ——————

If you've ever been on a hike and needed to jump over a creek, walk across a fallen tree, or hop over rocks, you know it's easier when someone is spotting you. Even if they aren't holding your hand to guide you across, their outstretched arms ensure you have the necessary support.

Waiting is full of these transitions, and they feel a lot scarier without a guide—someone who has been where we are and knows the territory. Isaiah 58:11 says, "Yahweh will always guide you where to go and what to do. He will fill you with refreshment even when you are in a dry, difficult place. He will continually restore strength to you, so you will flourish like a well-watered garden and like an ever-flowing, trustworthy spring *of blessing*."

Living It Out ❧ Often what scares us most is the pressure we feel to be our own guide through unfamiliar terrain. How would relying on God for guidance, comfort, and refreshment feel different for you? Journal what stands out to you.

Day 3 Prompt: Charting New Pathways

Neural pathways play vital roles in our brains. A neural pathway is "a series of connected neurons that send signals from one part of the brain to another. . . . These connected neurons process the information we receive. It is these that enable us to interact, as well as experience emotions and sensations. They create our memories and enable us to learn."[3]

Neural pathways are like paths in the woods. Each time these connected neurons fire, it's likened to someone walking a path in the woods. Every time we travel this path, the more defined and habitual it becomes.

When we're waiting and in transition, powerful shifts are happening—namely, we are creating new neural pathways in our brains. In other words, we are charting a new path in the woods. According to psychotherapist Ashley Mead, "The neural pathways that are built during big life transitions provide opportunity to develop new insights about the self."[4]

Transitions and waiting are so challenging partly because they are affecting change in our brains.

Living It Out ❧ Go on a walk, choosing a different path than you normally take. Notice how you feel choosing this path and how you can apply this new perspective to your current season.

•————— Day 4 Prompt: The Importance of Community —————•

I have been a part of the same small group since 2018. We never imagined we would become such integral parts of each other's lives. But almost four years later, the members remain some of my dearest friends.

Such gatherings provide the chance to gain new perspective. Each person who shares in community is like a diamond being turned to show another of its facets. These facets bring vital new perspectives and illuminate a path that community members may not have considered or known about.

Living It Out 🌿 How are you leaning on your community? What new perspectives have you gained from them? If you're hesitant in answering, do you need to broaden your circle and find a community that feels safe? Journal what comes to mind.

Light arises in the
darkness for the upright;
He is gracious and
compassionate and
righteous.

Psalm 112:4, AMP

SPRING

WATCHING AS WINTER GRADUALLY EVOLVES INTO SPRING reminds me of sitting in front of a warm fire after a day in the snow. The fire melts our shoulders into place and helps us regain feeling in our fingers and toes.

We have learned difficult lessons that only winter could teach us, and we are carrying fresh reserves of depth into spring. Barren trees begin to bud, and the warm breeze feels like a gentle embrace as we turn our tired faces toward the sun. The sun lingers and the days grow longer, and our collective mood lifts. We feel the possibilities around us and in us.

Waiting in spring comes with some advantages. Looking around and seeing physical representations of life after a cold, dormant winter, we feel a growing sense of hope: Not all is lost. We are not forgotten. Just when we were sure winter would last forever, the breeze warms, the bud breaks forth, and the sun soothes.

If winter is a marathon, spring is the finish line. Where there was once death, life rises up in new form: opportunities, revelations, and vision. Spring is undergirded by a hum of anticipation, a buzz of potential. "See, I am doing a new thing! Now it springs up; do you not perceive it? I am making a way in the wilderness" (Isaiah 43:19, NIV).

As we enter spring, we're reminded that the faith we held in other seasons was producing something wondrous all along. Spring invites us to take a breath as our hearts, minds, and bodies find restoration in the beauty bursting forth. Spring brings the rejuvenation we so desperately need. We may still be waiting for areas of our lives to blossom, but we feel strengthened by the hopeful possibilities of spring.

Straddling Two Worlds

Nothing before, nothing behind;
The steps of Faith
Fall on the seeming void, and find
The rock beneath.

JOHN GREENLEAF WHITTIER, "MY SOUL AND I"

AT TWENTY-NINE YEARS OLD, after spending most of my life on the East Coast, I left everything familiar and moved across the country. What scared me the most was leaving behind a future I understood. It felt like I was in the scene from *Alice in Wonderland* where Alice slides through a portal not knowing what new world she was headed into.

A week after arriving, my roommate and I visited a new church in the area. The Australian pastor started her message by sharing about having her first child.

She was nine months pregnant and began having contractions while teaching her college class. As soon as the contractions kicked in, so did the denial. She made it through her class, but instead of calling her husband and getting to the hospital, she went grocery shopping, came home, and put on a movie, trying to ignore the debilitating contractions. But when her husband came home, he found her on the floor doubled over in pain. When she arrived at the hospital, the doctor gave her the "You're about to have a baby" rundown, and she responded, "I think I should go home, get some rest, and then come back to have my baby." The doctor and nurses laughed, saying, "No, ma'am. You're having this baby now!"

The congregation laughed as well over her unusual reaction, and she added something I've never forgotten: Having her first child signaled a transition from the life she had known toward one that was completely unknown. She was stepping into a season foreign to her, losing her grip on a life she understood while not yet having a firm hold on the new life she was entering into. Straddling two worlds felt like she was losing control, and it was terrifying. Denial seemed like the best solution to silence the fear of the unknown.

When we wait, we straddle two worlds of hope and fulfillment, fear and faith. It can feel like a place of limbo where nothing feels steady. Fear spins convincing narratives, and we need confidence that what is uncharted and unfamiliar to us is well-known to God.

> Do not be afraid or discouraged, for the LORD will personally go ahead of you. He will be with you; he will neither fail you nor abandon you.
> DEUTERONOMY 31:8, NLT

When you are between the known and the unknown, God waits to be your bridge of comfort, hope, and strength.

Day 1 Prompt: Facing Reality

Denial is a powerful defense mechanism when we feel overwhelmed by reality. When we're waiting, we may slip into denial to silence the fear that tries to intimidate us with visions of dead ends and hopelessness.

We swing from fixating on our powerlessness over reality to denying it even exists. Neither option has the power to change anything, however. Instead, they drain us of precious time and energy. Denial vows to protect us, but in shielding us, it prevents us from growing in resilience and faith. Waiting for resolution in our stories involves many moments when we may tire of hoping and succumb to fear.

Living It Out 🌿 Listen to the song "You Make Me Brave" by Amanda Cook, and allow the lyrics to encourage you. Reflect on ways denial has vowed to protect you; then write them down and present them to God, asking him to make you brave in the unknown.

Day 2 Prompt: The Providence of God

When I was fourteen years old, I traveled to Thailand with my youth group. At the end of the trip, all thirty-five of us were on our way to the airport when I realized I had lost my passport.

My stomach dropped. The group needed to board the flight back to America, and since the airline could only guarantee one ticket for the following day, I had to stay behind.

Before the sun rose the next morning, the local pastor and I went to the place I remembered last having my passport—the king's palace. We arrived and were led by a guard down a dim, curvy hallway to a small room, where he grabbed a wicker basket and pulled out my passport. We were all shocked, including the guard. He explained that lost American passports were a hot commodity on the black market and usually sold to the highest bidder. A few hours later, I boarded my flight and flew home safely to my *very* worried parents.

As we're waiting, it's comforting to remember that God is faithful to go before us in situations that are out of our control. When you feel torn between fear and hope, you can rest knowing God is taking care of you in ways you cannot imagine.

Living It Out 🌿 Reflect on a time God providentially went before you while you were waiting. Journal about how this situation gives you hope to believe he will do it again.

Day 3 Prompt: Birthing Something Precious

When we're waiting, we often feel like we're birthing something precious, much like the Australian pastor.

There is a reason a woman waits nine months to have a baby. It takes that long for vital developments to take place within the mother and the child. This time prepares the mom mentally, emotionally, and physically, while also giving her baby time to fully develop.

Let endurance have its perfect result *and* do a thorough work, so that you may be perfect and completely developed [in your faith], lacking in nothing.

JAMES 1:4, AMP

While we're waiting, it's easy to lose sight of all that is being developed in and for us. We are growing many precious qualities—patience, character, love—that are preparing us for the external gifts God desires to give us.

Living It Out 🌿 With this perspective in mind, read the verse below, and write down what God is forming in you.

Just as you'll never understand the mystery of life forming in a pregnant woman, so you'll never understand the mystery at work in all that God does.

ECCLESIASTES 11:5, MSG

●————— **Day 4 Prompt: Perspective Is Everything** —————●

Sometimes it's difficult to see ourselves and our situations clearly. We're too close to them, and the pain can be blinding. Kind and honest perspectives from others can jump-start us out of denial and back into reality to help us through the hard parts.

Living It Out 🌿 Who do you trust to offer you a needed perspective? If no one readily comes to mind, ask God to highlight someone to you. Reach out to them and share what you have been learning about denial. Ask for their perspective, and pay attention to what resonates and encourages you.

Ditching the Formulas

Faith grows strong and vital in these thickets of uncertainty.
There is nothing clear or easy about the faith life.

TRICIA GATES BROWN

WHEN WE'RE WAITING, we want formulas: $A + B = C$. We want linear, predictable, and easy, not mysterious, hard, and uncertain.

Maybe, like me, you've often taken this formulaic approach with God. I had all kinds of formulas I would shuffle through to find one that worked. Each one was some version of "I will do this (A); God, you will do that (B); and Voilà! I get what I want! (C)"

God intends to answer our prayers, but his methods cannot be reduced to a formula. These formulaic messages creep into our theology and hypothetically shrink God to fit into our narrow boxes. They also reinforce a transactional approach with God: We "give to get" or "do to receive." That isn't a relationship; it's a business transaction. Anytime we make our relationships transactional, we set ourselves up for disappointment and resentment. But life with God is transformational, not transactional.

For so long I believed that if I did "good" things for God, he would have no choice but to answer my prayers. As a result, I found myself climbing out of painful holes of disappointment after my formula didn't get me the expected result.

What happens if God doesn't cooperate with our formulas? We get angry and resent him for not coming through for us. We blame him for not cooperating with the methods we concocted or working within the boxes we've built. So why do we keep doing this?

Linear thinking serves us in a lot of ways, especially in the realms of science and math. These fields operate on the relationship between cause and effect. According to an article in *Harvard Business Review*, decades of research show how our brains prefer to make simple straight lines to follow (i.e., A + B = C) and struggle to understand nonlinear relationships. [1]

One example of where nonlinear relationships come into play is open-ended questions. When I ask my clients open-ended questions, I am curiously inviting them into areas within themselves where there are no boxes or formulas. If anything, my clients are hoping to grow beyond disappointing formulas to a new place with God and themselves.

Choosing to bravely trust God and release our obsession with control frees us to discover a life beyond A + B = C. Our will and God's will are not in competition. They are more like partners in a dance. God honors our will, and we honor his. He desires to work in harmony with us for his purpose and our highest good.

Day 1 Prompt: Tapping into Your Expertise

I believe that each of my clients is as much of an expert as I am. They simply need space to slow down and a safe person who will listen and ask questions. Second Peter 1:3 says, "Everything we could ever need for life and godliness has already been deposited in us by his divine power." As Jesus followers, we not only have the Holy Spirit to guide us; we have also been created with the holy capacity to think, reason, and feel.

When I ask my clients open-ended questions, they are encouraged to consider something new. Trust the expertise God has deposited in you, and risk asking questions that may have no immediate answers.

Living It Out 🌿 Ask yourself, *What formula or box have I created, and why?* Ask God, *What is one characteristic you are developing in me as I wait? What fresh view do you want me to see?* Write down the answers that come to mind.

Day 2 Prompt: Challenging False Assumptions

Maybe you've heard touching stories about times when people gave money to God and miraculously received double in return. I believe in honoring

God with our finances, but sometimes these stories can communicate subtle misconceptions.

Without clarifying that we don't give to ensure that God returns the favor, we might think this is a formula for bending God's will to ours. Subtle but powerful messages such as this find their way into our theology, leaving us disappointed with God when we have done part *A*, but he hasn't fulfilled part *B* to give us *C*.

Living It Out ✎ What false assumptions have contributed to formulas about how God *should* be intervening in your life? Ask God to show you a new perspective on an old formula. Write down what comes to mind.

———— Day 3 Prompt: Radical Grace ————

Grace is radical because it's a gift we receive instead of something we earn. In his book *What's So Amazing about Grace?*, Philip Yancey talks about a conference years ago on comparative religions where experts debated what belief, if any, was unique to the Christian faith. Theologian C. S. Lewis responded confidently, "Oh, that's easy. It's grace." Yancey says that grace "seems to go against every instinct of humanity."[2]

Grace is the unmerited favor of God, unconditional love given to the undeserving. The formulas and boxes we create are in opposition to God's grace. Receiving grace feels vulnerable because we are surrendering to love and trusting God to care for us.

Living It Out ✎ How can you receive God's grace instead of grasping for control? Listen to Kari Jobe's rendition of "'Tis So Sweet to Trust in Jesus," and reflect on the chorus.

———— Day 4 Prompt: Shifting Our Focus ————

Genuinely helping others can be a powerful healing agent.

An article in *Greater Good Magazine* explains that a study showed how comforting others helps us with our own struggles. Participants interacted on a social network, sharing personal feelings of distress and responding to others in their distress. The platform trained them to leave comments of validation and reappraisal (offering a different interpretation of an event) and to point out thinking errors (i.e., black-and-white thinking).

Those who shared the most encouragement experienced the most improvement in their mood and symptoms. The researchers concluded that "helping [others] regulate their emotional reactions to stressful situations may be a particularly powerful way to practice and hone our own regulation skills."[3] Turning our focus to others can help heal our own hearts.

Living It Out 🌿 Do you know of someone who is navigating a waiting season? What is one way you can encourage them by using validation and reappraisal, as in the study?

Hope Is Dangerous

Your future is bright and filled with a living hope that will never fade away.

PROVERBS 23:18

HOPE FEELS DANGEROUS WHEN YOU'RE WAITING.

Our hearts are often more expectant of disappointment than they are of hope. We convince ourselves that the safest and most responsible course of action is to keep our expectations low, and that to align ourselves with hope would be to set ourselves up for sure disappointment.

During a difficult time in my life, I remember listening to a worship song with lyrics that confronted and surprised me: "You taught my feet to dance upon disappointment."[1] My eyes stung with hot tears because I desperately wanted to do that, but I had no idea how.

I felt like disappointment had won. I was armored up and committed to protect myself from hope. I thought I was in charge—empowered and safe— when in reality, this simple lyric showed me that disappointment had been dancing on me, not the other way around.

When we're afraid, we commonly manage our fear using self-protection. Some of the first discoveries I make with clients are their unique patterns for keeping themselves emotionally safe. Unfortunately, we don't realize the hidden costs of these patterns. We may be safe from risk and potential pain, but we are also "safe" from connection, intimacy, and belonging.

We need to revisit the parts in our stories where disappointment took root. Hope will always feel out of reach when disappointment plays like a bad-news loop in our heads.

The operative word in this worship song is *taught.* God is present with us as we revisit our past, and he's encouraging us to open our hearts to hope again. This isn't a skill we naturally have; it's one he imparts. As we experience healing, we are learning to dance on our disappointment—not the other way around.

━━━ Day 1 Prompt: Softening Our Heart toward Hope ━━━

One of my favorite movies is *The Shawshank Redemption*. Andy (played by Tim Robbins) and Red (played by Morgan Freeman) are convicts who become friends in prison, and both are serving life sentences. Andy has been falsely convicted of murder, and Red teaches him how to survive in prison.

In a scene where Andy is talking with other inmates, Red gets agitated and asks him, "What are you talking about?" Andy replies that he's talking about hope.

Red tells Andy, "Let me tell you something, my friend. Hope is a dangerous thing. Hope can drive a man insane."

At the close of the movie, Andy has escaped, and Red has been paroled, so he follows Andy's coded message to join him in Mexico. He boards a bus, and then the audience hears his inner thoughts as he leans out the window: "I'm so excited I can barely sit still or hold a thought in my head. I think it's the excitement only a free man can feel. . . . I hope I can make it across the border. I hope to see my friend and shake his hand. I hope the Pacific is as blue as it has been in my dreams. I *hope*."

Living It Out 🌿 The confinement of disappointment had taken its toll on Red, making him believe hope was dangerous. As he regained his freedom, his heart softened toward hope. If you feel confined by disappointment, ask God to remind you what's true about you and your future. Allow these truths to soften your heart to hope again.

━━━━━ Day 2 Prompt: Being Held ━━━━━

Disappointment is a powerful emotion, one we encounter often as we wait. We don't know how or when God will answer our prayers, so we do our best to trust him and take the risks he leads us to take. We may reach a point of feeling beat up by the wait, making the whole experience feel mysterious and unsettling. Richard Rohr says,

> The source of spiritual wisdom is to hold questions and contradictions patiently, much more than to find quick certitudes, to rush to closure or judgment. . . . A mature spiritual director will teach you how to negotiate the darkness, how to wait it out, how to hold on. . . . Whenever you choose or allow or surrender to the now, you can hold it in its entirety—the good and bad, the satisfying and unsatisfying, both what fulfills and what disappoints you. Saying *yes* to paradox positions you in a place that is bigger than your pain. . . . Here the Divine Friendship holds you.[2]

Living It Out 🌿 Listen to the song "Heroes" by Amanda Cook and allow the "Divine Friendship" to hold you. Journal what comes to mind.

Day 3 Prompt: A Costly Investment

Now, Lord, do it again! Restore us to our former glory! May streams of your refreshing flow over us until our dry hearts are drenched again. Those who sow their tears as seeds will reap a harvest with joyful shouts of glee.
PSALM 126:4-6

Your tears are an expensive investment, but the return will far outweigh the cost. It's similar to the experience a woman has when she delivers her baby. John 16:21-23 says, "When a woman gives birth, she has a hard time. . . . But when the baby is born, there is joy in the birth. This new life in the world wipes out memory of the pain. The sadness you have right now is similar to that pain, but the coming joy is also similar" (MSG).

Living It Out 🌿 Ask God to speak to you about tears you have sown and how they are softening the soil for a harvest of joy.

Day 4 Prompt: The Pitfall of Self-Protection

Brené Brown's work on shame and vulnerability provides essential language for seeing the value of vulnerability and exposing the shame that makes it challenging. In her book *Daring Greatly*, she discusses the frustration and disconnection we feel around someone who is "hidden or shielded by masks and armor." She highlights the paradox that "vulnerability is the last thing I want you to see in me, but the first thing I look for in you."[3]

Self-protection blocks us from connection with others. If we live hidden and shielded, we cut ourselves off from a lifeline of support and empathy from others. Our pain means we're human, and our vulnerability makes us strong.

Living It Out 🌿 Recall a time when someone was vulnerable with you and how it helped you feel less alone and more connected. Reach out to this person or someone you trust and share with them how you've been feeling recently.

Mindset Matters

*Our waiting is not nothing . . . because people tend to
be shaped by whatever it is they are waiting for.*

BARBARA BROWN TAYLOR, *GOSPEL MEDICINE*

THE WORDS *COMPLICATED* AND *COMPLEX* evoke distinctly different thoughts and
feelings. *Complicated* is defined as "difficult to analyze, understand, or explain,"[1]
while the definition for *complex* reads, "a whole made up of complicated or
interrelated parts."[2] The overlap in these definitions piqued my curiosity, so I
took an informal poll on social media, which yielded varied responses. I asked,

> Is there a major difference in your mind between the words *complex*
> and *complicated*?
> Does one feel more positive than the other? Which word feels more
> negative?

Responses included the following:

> "Complex equals intricate and layered, and complicated equals difficult."
> "Complex is more like a puzzle to solve; complicated implies an issue."
> "Complex invites exploration; complicated warns, 'I'm going to make
> you tired.'"
> "Complex has design, purpose, and order; complicated lacks order."

The article "The Critical Difference between Complex and Complicated"
discusses the words in a business context, but I was fascinated by how well the
insights translated into the experience of waiting. The author distinguishes

135

between a *complicated mindset* and a *complexity mindset*. Research showed that a complicated mindset is rigid and struggles with flexibility and adaptability. In contrast, a complexity mindset focuses on what can be, not just what is. It's creative, imaginative, flexible, and adaptive to unforeseen changes.[3]

A complicated mindset aims to fix and solve problems, whereas a complexity mindset thinks "manage, not solve."[4] A complicated mindset approaches life with an interest in certainty and control, but a complexity mindset approaches life with humility, possessing the willingness to embrace uncertainty and manage mystery.

God loves mystery and the word is mentioned in the New Testament twenty-eight times.[5]

> We continually speak of this wonderful wisdom that comes from God, hidden before now in a mystery.
>
> I CORINTHIANS 2:7

> He made known to us the mystery of his will according to his good pleasure, which he purposed in Christ.
>
> EPHESIANS 1:9, NIV

> This, then, is how you ought to regard us: as servants of Christ and as those entrusted with the mysteries God has revealed.
>
> I CORINTHIANS 4:1, NIV

So why is this relevant to our seasons of waiting? Waiting is mysterious and punctuated by both complication and complexity. Thankfully we aren't navigating any of this alone. God is with us in the mystery and is teaching us how to move through it.

Waiting is both "difficult to analyze, understand, and explain" and "made up of complicated and interrelated parts." And it's *how* we approach our waiting that determines our experience of it.

The humility of a complexity mindset enables us to *manage* uncertainty with God rather than try to solve it ourselves. In our spring seasons of waiting, may we learn how to hold space for complexities that feel mysterious, as well as complications that feel inconvenient, with confidence that we aren't navigating either alone.

•——————— **Day 1 Prompt: Growing Our Mindset** ———————•

Stanford psychologist Carol Dweck explains how we can live with one of two mindsets—fixed or growth:

"A fixed mindset believes the abilities that lead to success are static, and therefore further effort is not required. A growth mindset, on the other hand, believes abilities can be developed over time through effort and persistence: 'Either I'm good at it or I'm not' (fixed mindset) versus 'I can learn to do anything I want' (growth mindset)."[6]

When we approach waiting with a fixed and complicated mindset, we often feel stuck and hopeless. But a growth and complexity mindset motivates us to manage inevitable challenges.

Living It Out 🌿 Identify one way you can move toward a growth mindset. For example, if you've been telling yourself you're not good at taking risks, remind yourself that you can *learn* to take risks. Then take one small risk this week.

•——————— **Day 2 Prompt: Our Lives Are like a Tapestry** ———————•

The Hiding Place is an emotional memoir by Corrie ten Boom. Corrie and her sister were imprisoned and later sent to a concentration camp after they were caught hiding Jews in their home. Corrie often quoted a poem that has impacted me deeply, and I hope its perspective does the same for you:

My life is but a weaving, between my God and me. I cannot choose
the colors He weaveth steadily. Oft' times He weaveth sorrow; and
I in foolish pride forget He sees the upper and I the underside. Not
'til the loom is silent and the shuttles cease to fly will God unroll the
canvas and reveal the reason why. The dark threads are as needful
in the weaver's skillful hand as the threads of gold and silver in the
pattern He has planned.[7]

Living It Out 🌿 Reflect on how a tapestry's underside is tangled and messy, seemingly without form or beauty. The upper side is where order and intention can be seen. How does this perspective relate to your current season of waiting?

———— Day 3 Prompt: Curiosity versus Judgment ————

My friend Savannah is an avid researcher and shared some interesting information about curiosity and judgment. She learned that two different parts of our brains light up when we're being curious versus when we're being judgmental, rendering it impossible to be both at the same time. We need to choose.

Curiosity is akin to mystery. To accept mystery, we need to embrace curiosity. It takes curiosity to accept Jesus' invitation to join him by faith. As we approach our waiting with curiosity, we will be empowered to receive from God in ways not possible with judgment.

Living It Out 🌿 How can you choose curiosity over judgment today? Write down what comes to mind.

———— Day 4 Prompt: Seeing with Fresh Eyes ————

When I moved across the country, one of my first purchases was a new bed. I'll never forget opening the large box and looking at the directions and the fifteen bags of screws and debating whether I should sleep on an air mattress for the rest of my life.

Thankfully, my roommate swooped in, and after an hour, the bed was put together. Where I saw problems, she saw possibilities.

We need each other, especially in difficulties. Other people's fresh perspectives help us navigate the parts that feel complicated.

Living It Out 🌿 In what areas of your life are you seeing only problems you can't solve? Ask God to show you other people who can offer fresh perspectives. Are there others who might benefit from a similar gift of perspective from you?

See, I am doing a new
thing! Now it springs
up; do you not perceive
it? I am making a way
in the wilderness.

Isaiah 43:19, NIV

Your Doubt Is an Invitation

No matter how we rationalize, God will sometimes seem unfair
from the perspective of a person trapped in time.
PHILIP YANCEY, *DISAPPOINTMENT WITH GOD*

WHEN WE'RE WAITING, our relationship to time is complicated. We feel confined by time and trapped by our circumstances. And we acutely feel our lack of control over the timetable of our situation. Spring seasons of waiting can conjure up unexpected confusion as we watch the world around us come to life while our circumstances remain the same.

You've probably heard the saying "Perception is reality." It's only human to determine reality based on what we can see, hear, and feel. Our perception of a situation greatly influences our interpretation of it. The way we perceive God and ourselves during our season of waiting determines the reality in which we exist.

In Psalm 13:1-2, David candidly shares his questions about God's timing: "I'm hurting, Lord—will you forget me forever? How much longer, Lord? Will you look the other way when I'm in need? How much longer must I cling to this constant grief?"

As time dragged on, David grew tired and doubtful. His words reflect how confining waiting feels. Similar to grief, when you're in the lowest season of waiting, you cannot imagine a time when you won't feel sad. The present grief projects onto future possibilities.

Psychology professor Herbert L. Mirels, and researchers Paul Greblo and Janet B. Dean, reveal that those who experience chronic doubt are especially prone to mood swings, lower self-esteem, anxiety, and depression, and they express more discomfort with uncertainty. Mirels says they "might be more susceptible to depression because they often feel life is out of their control."[1]

The research confirms a truth many have experienced: Doubt weakens our resolve and drains us of much-needed strength. When doubt wreaks havoc on our hearts, we might assume it creates a wedge between God and ourselves. But I've learned that doubt is an invitation. Psalm 94:19 says, "When doubts filled my mind, your comfort gave me renewed hope and cheer" (NLT).

David knew his doubt didn't repel God; it attracted him. When we bring our doubts *to* God, we create opportunities to receive comfort, hope, and joy *from* God. David also knew that one of the most powerful remedies is worship. "I will sing my song of joy to you, Yahweh, for in all of this you have strengthened my soul. My enemies say that I have no Savior, but I know that I have one in you!" (Psalm 13:6).

With the measure of faith he possessed, he exchanged doubt for a resolve to praise. His resolution didn't mean his situation had changed. It simply meant he chose to align his perception of reality with the truth of God's promises. This choice is available to us, too, and it has the power to bring release to our hearts and minds and freedom within our waiting.

Day 1 Prompt: Can I Make Time Go Faster?

At the gym one day, my friend and I were doing sprints on the treadmill—which I affectionately refer to as an instrument of torture. Out of nowhere, an unexpected thought created a welcome interruption to the pain I felt in every part of my body: *I can't make time go by faster if I move faster.* My impatient brain irrationally thinks that if I move faster, time will speed up—as if I could affect time. Talk about "perception is reality."

Have you ever thought that if you did more, moved faster, were a better person, were *enough*, that your waiting would end? That time would speed up, getting you closer to fulfilled desires? We place a lot of conditions on when and how our waiting will end. What if today you release the conditions and accept yourself exactly where you are? I'm not talking about resignation; I'm talking about an acceptance that brings peace.

Living It Out 🌿 Journal about releasing these conditions. Afterward, notice what feels different—your relationship with God, your current situation, and most importantly, yourself.

—— Day 2 Prompt: Your Perceptions of God ——

Perceptions are powerful, and we are loyal to them. It is an exercise in humility to consider what possibilities could exist outside our immediate perception of a situation. To that end, here are a number of questions to reflect on as you journal today:

What negative perceptions have I held about God in relation to waiting?
Have I perceived God as unkind, passive, and neglectful?
What specific experiences have contributed to these perceptions?

Living It Out 🌿 How does holding this view of God influence your current reality? What feels possible or impossible because of these perceptions?

—— Day 3 Prompt: How Doubt Feels ——

What does doubt feel like to you? In other words, how would you describe it to someone? I often incorporate experiential techniques to help clients move from their head to their heart.

For example, once they identify their strongest emotion, I place a handful of scarves in front of them, scarves with different colors, textures, and patterns. Then I direct them to choose a scarf that best represents what that emotion feels like. If they identify doubt, perhaps they choose a red scarf with a chaotic pattern, explaining that their doubt resembles anger and makes them feel confused. The more precise language we can use to describe how we feel, the more specific we can be with God when we invite him into it.

Living It Out 🌿 Grab some scarves or pick an item that reflects your feelings of doubt. Write down what you notice about it and your doubt. Pray and invite God into this place with you, noticing his compassion toward you.

Day 4 Prompt: Your Doubt Doesn't Disqualify You (or Anyone Else)

It is both comforting and intriguing to me that Thomas, one of Jesus' disciples, is dubbed "doubting Thomas."

I'm also encouraged that his doubt did not exclude or disqualify him from being in Jesus' closest community. Not only was Jesus unintimidated by Thomas's doubts; so were his closest friends. How can you be encouraged by this reality and quick to extend your friendship to others who are doubting?

Jesus saw Thomas's doubt as an invitation. In John 20:24-28, the disciples are gathered together, and Thomas says, "Unless I see the nail marks in his hands and put my finger where the nails were, and put my hand into his side, I will not believe" (NIV). Jesus later makes an appearance, walking through the wall of their meeting place and asking Thomas to touch the wound in his side and look at his nail-scarred hands.

Living It Out 🌿 What have you been asking God to show you in order to help you believe he is for you in the waiting? Close your eyes and imagine that God is there with you. Share what you have been doubtful about, and notice how he responds. Journal what stands out to you.

The Messy Middle

Trust: In these wild and new unknowns, your story is still taking shape.
MORGAN HARPER NICHOLS

THE COMMON THREAD IN ANY GREAT STORY is always a strong narrative arc. One of the important components of this is an "inciting incident." The conflict, tension, and discomfort resulting from this incident lead to a key moment when the main character makes an important decision.

As we step into the character's story, we are bearing witness to their struggle. The hope for resolve keeps us on the edge of our seats—committed to seeing the story through to the end. As the character wrestles with their questions and pain, we're given an opportunity to wrestle with our own. We resonate with the tension-filled middle because we are familiar with its weight and agitation.

I always knew how powerful storytelling was, but it wasn't until grad school that I realized why. In one of my classes, I took an assessment called the Clifton StrengthsFinder, which helps individuals discover their top strengths. I learned that one of mine is *connectedness*. Those with connectedness see events, interpersonal interactions, and emotional elements coming together to create a beautiful picture that could never be formed alone.

Connectedness is a hardwiring to look for the dots in order to connect them. This eye for connection enables me to listen for unspoken longings in my client's stories. We gather the information and string it together, putting each piece in its proper place. This process allows something powerful to happen: My client not only sees how much their story makes sense, but also how much *they* make sense in context of it.

Our hopes and desires to connect the dots of our stories make waiting profoundly difficult. Hebrews 11:1 says, "Now faith brings our hopes into reality and becomes the foundation needed to acquire the things we long for. *It is all the evidence required to prove what is still unseen*" (emphasis mine).

You know the key moment in the narrative arc we talked about—the one when the main character makes an important choice? As we're walking through the messy middle of waiting, we are faced with the critical choice to believe that no matter how our circumstances appear, God has not forgotten us or abandoned us.

It's easy to assume that the ultimate moment in our stories is when we receive long-awaited answers to prayers. But it is just as monumental when we trust that the evidence of our prayers exists even if we haven't seen it yet. These are the true culminating moments in our stories—ones when *we* change before our circumstances do.

God is the best weaver of compelling stories, and he is committed to bringing you and your story to completion. Don't be surprised when the process is full of tension, doubt, and confusion. Rest assured, knowing that God makes everything beautiful and complete in its time (Ecclesiastes 3:11).

•——— Day 1 Prompt: Choosing Hope over Disappointment ———•

We Are Marshall is one of my favorite movies. It chronicles the true story of the Marshall University football team after a 1970 plane crash claimed the lives of seventy-five people on board, including team members, staff, and many fans.

Matthew McConaughey plays Jack Lengyel, a coach at a different college who is deeply moved when he hears about the plane crash and is hired to take on the challenging job of head coach at Marshall. The story follows him building a new team to restore hope to a hurting town.

Through their pain, the players ban together and work hard to rebuild their team. The climactic moments in the story happen just as much when the characters choose hope over disappointment as when they have unexpected victories on the field as a new team.

Living It Out 🌿 Write down how your story may parallel theirs. Although the circumstances may be different, consider how choosing hope over disappointment changed the Marshall team and gave them courage to see unlikely victories. Consider how your choices can do the same in your life.

Day 2 Prompt: Stories Are God's Idea

The Bible is proof of how much God loves storytelling. Dan Taylor says, "Stories are God's idea. God is the one who created story—the form of story—and us as story-shaped creatures. He has chosen story as the primary way to present himself to his creation."[1]

Stories are one of God's ways to connect with us, so they must be an impactful conduit to reach our hearts. Which story in the Bible about waiting resonates with you? Hannah, who waited for a baby (1 Samuel 1)? David, who waited to be king of Israel (2 Samuel 5)? Or Jacob, who waited to marry Rachel (Genesis 29)?

Living It Out 🌿 Read one of these stories, or another that resonates with you, and notice the transformations and climactic moments taking place in them as the characters waited to receive the desires of their hearts.

Day 3 Prompt: The Seasons Tell the Best Stories

The physical seasons tell the most dramatic stories. Think about it: In fall the foliage erupts into shades of yellow, orange, pink, and red. The air cools, reminding us to prepare for change. As the richly colored leaves slowly dance to the ground, we hear the sounds of the season shift to minor chords, bringing a soberness to our mood.

In winter, the world becomes cold and barren. The sky releases magical white powder, making even the most unseemly thing beautiful. In spring, the seasonal music changes again, lifting our spirits. The world thaws, and the trees sprout buds that burst into blooms. Summer crashes in like fireworks, exploding with adventure. The days stretch long, and we close our evenings with fireflies dancing about and loved ones by our side.

Tell me you didn't hear the most beautiful and complex story in that? God is the best storyteller, and he loves to speak to us through the seasons.

Living It Out 🌿 Close your eyes and imagine your favorite season. Notice the story that God wants to tell you through it about your season of waiting.

—————— Day 4 Prompt: The Cast in Your Story Matters ——————

We are not the only character in our stories—imagine how boring that would be, like in the movie *Cast Away*, where Tom Hanks is shipwrecked on an island alone, save a volleyball he affectionally calls Wilson.

The cast in our stories matters—especially to God. He's made no mistake when it comes to the people you are journeying through life with. They have so much to add, and likewise, you have so much to add to their lives.

Living It Out 🌿 When we are preoccupied with what or who we desire in the future, we lose sight of the people in our stories now. Reflect on who they are. If you feel compelled, reach out and share how thankful you are for their presence.

False Starts

Trust God from the bottom of your heart; don't try to figure out everything on your own. Listen for God's voice in everything you do, everywhere you go.

PROVERBS 3:5-6, MSG

WAITING INVOLVES FALSE STARTS: moments when you think, *It's time, and I'm ready*—only to realize later that it was a false start.

There are two kinds of false starts: ones where you take a risk without much deliberation and realize not every leap achieves the desired result, and others where you step out after much consideration, confident that God is in support, only for it to unravel before your eyes. This tension is common in the spring seasons of waiting—situations will appear promising, but we cannot know for sure if they will yield the desired result.

A few summers ago, I had one of those false-start moments. I took a bold step toward a promising situation, only to watch it come to a screeching halt. In my confusion, I went for a walk to pray and make sense of an opportunity that had once seemed so full of potential.

As I talked with God, I felt him gently adjust my heart as he brought the story of Joseph to mind. In the Bible, Joseph was the dreamer who was sold to slave traders by his brothers because of their jealousy. And to make matters worse, he was later thrown into prison because of a false accusation.

While in prison, Joseph was asked by two other prisoners to interpret their dreams. Joseph replied, "Do not interpretations belong to God? Tell me your dreams" (Genesis 40:8, NIV).

Then Pharaoh had a dream no one could interpret, so Joseph was summoned. "I had a dream last night, and no one here can tell me what it means.

But I have heard that when you hear about a dream you can interpret it'" (Genesis 41:15, NLT).

Standing before Pharaoh, Joseph spoke clearly about who actually holds the power to interpret dreams. "'It is beyond my power to do this,' Joseph replied. 'But God can tell you what it means and set you at ease'" (Genesis 41:16, NLT).

Joseph refused to take the interpretation into his own hands and instead listened to Pharaoh tell him about his dream. Then he offered it back to God for *his* interpretation.

Joseph's story is an example of someone who sought God and waited for his interpretation rather than taking it upon himself to make sense of what was happening. He resisted the urge to rely on assumptions and instead looked to God for understanding.

We make assumptions either out of pride—we think we know better—or ignorance—we don't know any better. But God wants something more for us. He wants us to live with humility and slow down long enough to offer a promise or dream back to God for his interpretation.

False starts are a normal, albeit painful, part of taking risks and moving in faith. False starts are simply *premature* starts, and that is what makes them unsuccessful—not your attempt, effort, or desire. It's the timing.

As you wait, keep your ears and heart set on God until the day the timing is right. It will be the start you have believed for, and you will be proud of yourself for listening, leaning in, and not giving up.

Day 1 Prompt: Choosing Curiosity

Curiosity about why we assume so much led me to some research from a Yale neurobiology professor. The brain's neural network requires a lot of energy to keep it running, so to save energy, our brain encodes information. One of the ways it does so is by assuming.[1]

We draw on past experiences to find patterns for how the world works, and when we encounter something new, we apply these assumptions. For example, if I already know what kinds of clothes are appropriate at work, I lean on that assumption to avoid using extra brain power.

What makes assumption problematic is the belief that our assumptions are the only right explanation. The antidote offered in the research is *curiosity*. I believe curiosity and humility go hand in hand and make each other possible.

Living It Out 🌿 Write down some of your assumptions about your season of waiting. Then write down a statement or question beside each one that reflects a sense of curiosity as you consider other interpretations.

———— Day 2 Prompt: Creating Space to Listen ————

When we create space for God, he will always show up and fill it. As mentioned in this week's devotional, when I was confused about one of my own false starts, I decided to take a walk and pray, and God showed up in a way that changed me. In Matthew 7:7-8, Jesus reminds us,

> *Keep on* asking, and you will receive what you ask for. *Keep on* seeking, and you will find. *Keep on* knocking, and the door will be opened to you. For everyone who asks, receives. Everyone who seeks, finds. And to everyone who knocks, the door will be opened (NLT, emphasis mine).

The words *keep on* speak to the importance of persistence. Waiting is energy-sucking, and persistence may feel daunting. But every time we ask, seek, and knock, God shows up—rarely as we think he will, but always in a way that leaves us better.

Living It Out 🌿 Take time this week to walk and talk with God. Share your thoughts with him, and leave space for him to speak. It may take some time to hear him clearly, so find rest in the promises of Matthew 7:7-8.

———— Day 3 Prompt: God's Invitation to Go Deeper ————

I have had many conversations with friends and clients about their confusion when promises they believed were from God didn't come to pass.

I once heard a preacher talk about Jesus' response to hearing that Lazarus was sick. In John 11:4, Jesus says, "This sickness will not end in death. No, it is for God's glory so that God's Son may be glorified through it" (NIV). But it was a statement that Lazarus's sisters presumably didn't hear or possibly understand. Can you imagine Mary's and Martha's confusion when Lazarus dies?

We might assume that Jesus' words meant Lazarus would be spared from death, but Jesus actually said his sickness would not *end* in death. It's important we don't stop short in discerning the meaning of his words. God isn't trying to trick us when he speaks; he is inviting us to go deeper with him.

Living It Out 🌿 What promises and dreams have you felt confused about because they didn't unfold as you imagined? Write down one, and ask God to show you something new about it.

•——————— **Day 4 Prompt: Taking the Time to Process** ———————•

Talking with a therapist or friend and journaling are helpful for many reasons. For starters, they allow us to take what is internal and make it external. Whenever we journal or verbally process with someone, issues that felt big feel much smaller.

Research from UCLA suggests that putting your feelings into words—a process called "affect labeling"—reduces the intensity of our emotional reactions to stress.[2] And research from Southern Methodist University suggests that writing about traumatic experiences and talking with a therapist positively impacted patients' health and immune systems.[3]

It's important to process what lives in our minds and hearts. Many assumptions can be avoided when we organize our thoughts on a page or let someone we trust into our process.

Living It Out 🌿 What thoughts that feel big would be helpful to process with someone you trust? Write them down along with the person's name you may share with this week.

The Great Contradiction

Wait. This was the first lesson I had learned about love.
ATTRIBUTED TO PAULO COELHO

I HAVE READ LAZARUS'S STORY MANY TIMES during seasons of waiting. In John 11, we read of Lazarus's sisters sending a message to Jesus about their sick brother. Upon receiving it, Jesus announces that Lazarus's sickness will not end in death. What he does next holds an element of mystery still today.

> Now Jesus loved Martha and her sister and Lazarus. So when he
> heard that Lazarus was sick, *he stayed* where he was two more days.
> JOHN 11:5-6, NIV, EMPHASIS MINE

As the story unfolds, Jesus makes another announcement: "Our friend Lazarus has fallen asleep; but I am going there to wake him up" (verse 11, NIV). Then Jesus says something that probably sent shockwaves through everyone who heard it. "Lazarus is dead, and for your sake I am glad I was not there, so that you may believe. But let us go to him" (verses 14-15, NIV).

Jesus' actions appear confusing. Why wouldn't he hurry to spare them pain?

It's normal to gauge someone's love *for you* based on their behavior *toward you*, and to assume internal affections are revealed by outward actions. This story challenges this fundamental perception.

Have you experienced contradictions between God's actions and his declaration of love for you? I have many times.

Disappointments and delays threaten to undermine our confidence in

God's love. Normally, we think love rushes to help. So when God seems to neglect and ignore us, we feel rejection more than love.

When Jesus shows up, *four days late*, we understand Martha's heartache. She tells Jesus that if he had only come on time, her brother wouldn't have died. And Martha is right; Jesus doesn't even correct her. Instead, he walks to Lazarus's tomb and mourns the loss of his friend.

Even the onlookers wonder at his seeming inaction. "Could not he who opened the eyes of the blind man have kept this man from dying?" (verse 37, NIV). Yes, they're right too. He could have come when he was summoned and kept this man from dying. But he didn't. Ultimately, we see Jesus calling Lazarus out of his tomb and raising his sick friend back to life.

The reason Jesus did not prevent Lazarus's death changes everything we know about God and his love. We're challenged to reconsider many concepts about him, namely how God's love prioritizes his glory and wants to give us something greater than we expected. But these gifts come at a cost, and one of them is waiting.

What is true of Lazarus's story is true of yours—significant gifts are at stake in your waiting. If God appears unloving, it's because he is expanding your understanding to include a love that is committed to giving you something greater *through* your difficult experiences of waiting.

Day 1 Prompt: Don't Stop Short

"Don't stop short." I say this to clients a lot. Stopping short often leads to taking situations at face value when so much more is going on below the surface. As we see beyond our circumstances, we gain valuable insight.

Psalm 25:14 says, "Friendship with God is reserved for those who reverence him. With them alone he shares the secrets of his promises" (TLB). It's easy to stop short at the frustrations and inconveniences of waiting, but there is so much God wants to show us during these difficult seasons.

Living It Out 🌿 What part of your waiting have you been taking at face value? Write down what comes to mind (and don't stop short). Talk with God like you would a friend, and listen for his reply. His response may come in many forms (a memory, a song, a verse), so accept it in whatever way it comes.

Day 2 Prompt: Breaking Character

This week's devotional reminds me of the Canaanite woman who came to Jesus for the sake of her demon-possessed daughter (Matthew 15:21-28). Jesus' response to her desperate plea is shocking, almost offensive. At first, he ignores her cries for help. Then he seems to reject her: "I was sent only to the lost sheep of Israel" (verse 24, NIV). Finally, when she falls in front of him pleading, "Lord, help me!" (verse 25, NIV), Jesus says, "It is not right to take the children's bread and toss it to the dogs" (verse 26, NIV).

If this were me, I would have felt shame envelop me before rushing out of there. Yet this woman doesn't cower in shame but responds to Jesus with audacious confidence. "'Yes it is, Lord,' she said. 'Even the dogs eat the crumbs that fall from their master's table'" (verse 27, NIV).

Jesus seems to "break character" when he hears her deep declaration of faith. "'Woman, you have great faith! Your request is granted.' And her daughter was healed at that moment" (verse 28, NIV). This is another powerful example of how Jesus' actions seem to contradict his loving nature at first, yet for a purpose—so our faith has a chance to grow and express itself.

Living It Out 🌿 Consider how the Canaanite woman's story parallels your own experience of waiting. Journal what stands out to you.

Day 3 Prompt: Different Kinds of Love

There are four different Greek words for love, including *storgē* (family love), *erōs* (romantic love), *philia* (friend love), and *agapē* (unconditional love).

Agapē love is the essence of who God is, and the quality and depth of God's love informs his "ways." "My ways are far beyond anything you could imagine. For just as the heavens are higher than the earth, so my ways are higher than your ways and my thoughts higher than your thoughts" (Isaiah 55:8-9, NLT).

There will be many times during our seasons of waiting when God's ways will appear different and confusing to us. But we can rest in the truth that God's love is behind the ways he works in our lives.

Living It Out 🌿 The apostle Paul's prayer for the church in Ephesus holds true for us today: "Being rooted and established in love, may [you] have power . . . to grasp how wide and long and high and deep is the love of Christ, and to know this love that surpasses knowledge" (Ephesians 3:17-19, NIV). What does "being rooted" in God's love mean to you? How can this rooting help you better understand God's ways? Write down what comes to mind.

———— Day 4 Prompt: The Language of Love ————

I have been gifted with incredible friends, and Lisa and Grace are two of my closest. I've known Grace for twenty-four years and Lisa for sixteen. They have seen me at my worst and have also celebrated with me at my best.

You may have friends such as these, with whom you can be unfiltered, unreserved, and unqualifying. It takes time to learn about each other since we all express love uniquely. We don't always recognize another person's words or actions as loving. Learning the heart of love behind the actions is worth the time.

Living It Out 🌿 Who has been an example of unconditional love to you? Write down some of their characteristics and how they have impacted you. Don't hesitate to share your thoughts with whomever came to mind. Let them know you appreciate how they have loved you so well.

Your future is bright
and filled with a living
hope that will never
fade away.

Proverbs 23:18

God Fills Empty Things

The answer lies in developing the capacity
to accept the finite disappointment
and yet cling to the infinite hope.

MARTIN LUTHER KING, JR.,
THE PAPERS OF MARTIN LUTHER KING, JR., VOLUME VI

WHEN I MEET A CLIENT FOR THE FIRST TIME, I typically ask what brings them to see me. Their eyes widen (because it feels impossible to summarize everything); then they inhale deeply and exhale some version of "I feel stuck, frustrated, and hopeless."

After one of these first sessions, I thought of the time when Jesus borrows Peter's fishing boat. I wasn't sure why this story came to mind, but it felt significant, so I opened my Bible app and found it.

The story begins with Jesus surrounded by hundreds of people clamoring for his attention; then he notices two fishing boats left vacant by some disappointed fishermen. Jesus commandeers their boat so the crowd can hear him, and before we know it, the focus shifts as Jesus directs his attention to these fishermen, who were washing their nets.

> "Put out into the deep water and lower your nets for a catch [of fish]." Simon [Peter] replied, "Master, we worked hard all night [to the point of exhaustion] and caught nothing [in our nets], but at Your word I will [do as you say and] lower the nets [again]."
>
> LUKE 5:4-5, AMP

They'd worked all night, only to pull up empty nets over and over again. This is how waiting feels. We pray and believe, sometimes to the point of emotional and physical exhaustion, only to come up empty-handed.

I hear tender stories every day from clients who feel emptied of hope and full of disappointment. This emptiness is often what compels them to seek help.

Peter and his fellow fishermen did something very normal—they left their boats to wash their nets. But until recently I never noticed that when they left their *empty* boats to wash their *empty* nets, they created a space for Jesus, the hope of the world, to fill their boats and hearts with himself.

Disappointment can leave us feeling empty-handed and empty-hearted. But what if it's actually carving out space and eliciting an invitation for God to fill those places with himself?

I saw myself in Peter's response and heard my own words reflected in his.

"I've tried."
"I've prayed."
"I've believed."
"I've waited . . . and nothing has changed."

Jesus' instructions weren't very practical. Peter, an experienced fisherman, knew that fish are most active at night because of cooler water temperatures, so it was unlikely they would catch fish in the middle of the day. Even so, Jesus instructs Peter to take those freshly washed nets and climb back into his boat and try *again.*

As the story goes, "When they had done this, they caught a great number of fish, and their nets were [at the point of] breaking" (Luke 5:6, AMP). This story offers a healing perspective for hearts that are hopeless and tired of waiting. Hearts that feel forgotten and are longing for the fulfillment of long-awaited desires.

Whatever proverbial boat you have left vacant and whatever nets you are washing—Jesus is waiting *there.* He is waiting to step into the empty space your disappointment left behind. He is waiting to encourage you to go again, believe again, trust him again.

Day 1 Prompt: A Powerful Force for Connection

Emotional attunement is a powerful force for connection. It's defined as "the ability to recognise, understand and engage with another's emotional state."[1]

Emotional attunement is essential to feeling connected to our primary caregivers. This attunement also assists in brain development and teaches us how to self-regulate. When someone is emotionally attuned to you, they are empathizing with you—feeling what you're feeling.

Jesus' attunement to Peter's disappointment creates a powerful opportunity for connection and transformation. Peter is forever changed after his encounter with Jesus, and when we experience this attunement from Jesus, it changes us too.

Living It Out 🌿 Close your eyes and imagine yourself in a safe place with Jesus. Notice what it's like for Jesus to be attuned to how you're feeling. Don't be surprised if it brings up mixed emotions. Stay in this place as long as you need to; then write down what stood out to you.

Day 2 Prompt: Go Out Where It Is Deeper

The NLT version of Luke 5:4, "Now go out where it is deeper," reminds me of Psalm 107:23-24: "Those who go down to the sea in ships, who do business on great waters; they have seen the works of the Lord, and His wonders in the deep" (AMP).

When we accept the invitation to go deeper, we experience God in our waiting like never before. This depth is a gift, but it requires brave steps into unfamiliar places. Be comforted in knowing that God only invites us into places where he promises to be present with us.

Living It Out 🌿 What scares you about going "out where it is deeper"? What does this deeper place represent to you? Write down what comes to mind.

Day 3 Prompt: Choosing to Be Brave

I remember reading Habakkuk 3:17-18 during a difficult time and being torn between inspiration and sadness.

Even though the fig trees have no blossoms, and there are no grapes on the vines; even though the olive crop fails, and the fields lie empty and barren; even though the flocks die in the fields, and the cattle barns are empty, yet I will rejoice in the LORD! I will be joyful in the God of my salvation! (NLT)

When Habakkuk penned these words, the Jewish people were experiencing painful oppression by the Babylonians. This declaration of surrender is nestled within dismal circumstances. It is humbling to read the repeated words *even though*. Similar to Peter lowering the nets again at Jesus' invitation, Habakkuk says, even here, *I will trust you.*

Living It Out 🌿 What are some difficult words of surrender you could say to God? Write down these words and the reasons why they feel difficult to say.

——— Day 4 Prompt: Sharing in Each Other's Grief *and* Joy ———

Romans 12:15 says, "Rejoice with those who rejoice [sharing others' joy], and weep with those who weep [sharing others' grief]" (AMP).

We are deeply connected, and our experiences as we wait profoundly impact those around us. Richard Wurmbrand was a Romanian Lutheran minister who, because of his faith, was imprisoned for fourteen years in Romania. In his memoir, *Tortured for Christ*, he recalls that he got so sick he was thrown into the "dying room," where no one survived more than a few days. But he continued to share his faith in this death room for more than two years. Countless prisoners he shared Christ with passed away, while he miraculously stayed alive to continue sharing his faith with others.[2]

Although our waiting may not be life or death, Wurmbrand is an astounding example of someone who, even in pain, chose to connect with others in theirs.

Living It Out 🌿 How can you share in someone's grief and joy this week? Could you send flowers or a card? Or simply send a text or make a call? Write down what comes to mind.

The Anniversary Effect

I know I will live to see how kind you are.
PSALM 27:13, CEV

WHEN WE'RE IN A SEASON OF WAITING, birthdays, anniversaries, and holidays often drum up painful emotions. Grief, sadness, disappointment, and loneliness can show up unannounced and unwelcomed.

The term for this experience is the *anniversary effect*. It is "a collection of disturbing feelings, thoughts or memories that occur on or around a date that marks a significant event."[1] We experience the anniversary effect just as much when something has *not* happened as when something *has*.

These anniversaries are painful reminders that we are still waiting. Our arms and hearts are still waiting to hold the tangible fulfillment of our desires. Although our desires may be different, we share in the difficult experience of yearly anniversaries that ping our hearts with sadness.

The anticipation of these anniversaries is often more painful than the day itself. Some of my hardest moments have been leading up to a birthday or New Year's, when I would turn another year older or begin another new year without tangible answers to my prayers. All of us process our pain differently, but I've learned how unbearable and unnecessary it is to carry the weight of grief alone.

> Carry one another's burdens and in this way you will fulfill the requirements of the law of Christ [that is, the law of Christian love].
> GALATIANS 6:2, AMP

There have been many birthdays and holidays when friends and family have rallied around me with parties, heartfelt cards, and kind gestures. When it was difficult to receive comfort from God, I felt his love through those around me.

> Let me give you a new command: Love one another. In the same way I loved you, you love one another. This is how everyone will recognize that you are my disciples—when they see the love you have for each other.
>
> JOHN 13:35, MSG

We all know what it's like to feel afraid, confused, and alone. It's hard to see at first, but we are given rich opportunities to love and be loved by others while we wait. Allowing each other into the process makes us feel vulnerable, but it also creates moments to celebrate with one another when our character deepens and long-awaited prayers are answered.

We aren't seeking out pain, but we are seeking the purpose veiled within it. Pain is an unlikely gift, one that empowers us to empathize with others in a way we never could without it. Believe me, I don't love this idea, but that doesn't mean it's not true. As we wait and courageously lean in to the purpose of this season, we will continue to see how kind God is to transform us and give us something beautiful to share with the world that has the power to transform them too.

Day 1 Prompt: Preparation over Anticipation

One of the hardest parts about the anniversary effect is the anticipation. Our assumptions about how we'll feel create anticipatory anxiety. This form of anxiety is different from other forms because it is a reaction to what we perceive as an "unpredictable threat."[2]

When we don't know what to expect, we project fearful possibilities and make up stories to fill in the gaps. This causes anticipatory anxiety to grow and become bigger than the actual pain on the anniversary. Rather than bracing and anticipating, we need to learn how to prepare our minds, hearts, and spirits from a place of *peace* rather than fear.

Living It Out 🌿 *Prepare your mind* by bringing awareness to the stories you're telling yourself. Write down these stories, and talk with a friend about this upcoming anniversary.

Prepare your body by going for a walk, to a yoga class, or on a hike. Engage in movement that feels restorative, and take cleansing breaths to release anxiety you've been holding in your body.

Prepare your heart by writing down the emotions you've been feeling: grief, disappointment, loneliness, etc. Close your eyes, and reflect about what these emotions are telling you about your needs. If you're feeling lonely, perhaps you need connection. If you're feeling disappointed, maybe you need encouragement.

Day 2 Prompt: God Is In Your Tomorrow

I've always found it interesting that we are subject to time, bound by the twenty-four hours we're living in and directly impacted by what does or doesn't happen during that time. Mysteriously, God exists outside of time and is not bound by it. Second Peter 3:8 says, "With God, one day.is as good as a thousand years, a thousand years as a day" (MSG).

When it comes to how time impacts us, it's reassuring to know that God is as present with us now as when an anniversary comes. "Do not be afraid or discouraged, for the LORD will personally go ahead of you. He will be with you; he will neither fail you nor abandon you" (Deuteronomy 31:8, NLT).

Living It Out 🌿 God is in your tomorrow. He knows what it holds and promises to be faithful to you. What anniversary are you dreading? Close your eyes and see that God is already there with you. It's okay if you can't see or feel God's presence right away; be reassured that sometimes it takes time to settle into seeing God in this way. Notice how he is providing for you and the ways he wants to comfort you. Write down what comes to mind.

Day 3 Prompt: Getting Honest with God

It's challenging to keep our hearts soft toward God when circumstances haven't changed. Being honest with God is hard for many of us, perhaps because of misguided ideas that we need to keep up appearances with him, or that it would somehow be dishonoring if we told him what we *really* thought.

The Psalms are encouraging because the psalmists don't hold back from God. Sometimes seeing someone else be honest gives us permission to do the same.

Living It Out 🌿 Read Psalm 6 in *The Message* version, and allow it to give you permission to be honest with God. Talk with him about how you feel and what you need from him today.

•——— Day 4 Prompt: Waiting Feels Less Heavy with a Friend ———•

Fascinating research from the University of Virginia reveals how differently we experience pain when we have a trusted friend nearby.

Participants wearing heavy backpacks stood at the bottom of a steep hill. During the first round of the study, they were alone and asked to rate the hill's steepness. Then the researchers asked the same participants, wearing the same backpacks, to rate the steepness again, but this time alongside a trusted friend. The results were telling. Every participant rated the hill as less steep when their friend was near.[3] We are important to each other, especially when life is heavy and the road looks steep.

Living It Out 🌿 Close your eyes and imagine standing at the bottom of a steep hill carrying the heaviness of your waiting. Notice what it feels like to stand there alone. Then imagine someone you trust there with you, and how it feels different. Write down what stands out to you, and who this person is standing beside you.

Living Wholeheartedly While You Wait

*Our captors tormented us, saying, "Make music for us
and sing one of your happy Zion-songs!" But how could we
sing the song of the Lord in this foreign wilderness?*

PSALM 137:3-4

AT THIS POINT IN HISTORY, the children of Israel had been torn from their homes and taken into captivity. Their captors demanded a song of celebration, but they couldn't imagine singing this melody while in the most devastating season of their lives.

Waiting is its own form of captivity. We feel confined mentally, emotionally, and even physically by circumstances outside our control—and we still have lives to lead while our hearts long for release. Work tasks need to be completed, dinners need to be made, children need to be taken care of . . . all while we're carrying the heaviness of waiting.

We're torn between sadness and the need to keep moving forward. In these conflicting moments, we ask ourselves a question similar to the one that was asked of the Israelites: *How do we live wholeheartedly today when we feel trapped by the pain of unfulfilled desires?*

As a therapist, the word *trapped* comes up a lot. Feeling trapped is an overwhelming experience that is either a response to present trauma or the echo of one from the past. Panic rises as our sense of power slips through our fingers. This real or imagined loss of control makes an experience feel traumatic.

There will always be factors outside our control that influence our waiting—like when your partner refuses to change their hurtful behavior and it's impacting your relationship. Or when no matter what you've tried, every pregnancy test comes back negative.

How do we find relief when circumstances haven't changed? How do we live wholeheartedly while waiting? We assume the remedy is to gain mastery over our circumstances, without realizing that our attempts to regain control over factors we cannot control only lead to feeling more trapped.

In *The Book of Awakening*, Mark Nepo says, "If we don't feel our feelings all the way through, they never leave us, and we do all kinds of unusual things to get out from under them. Though we fear it, feeling our feelings is the only clear and direct way to free our hearts of pain."[1]

The first step to finding relief is to acknowledge we feel trapped. Voicing our feelings brings a profound sense of freedom. Start each day by reminding yourself of everything you *do* have control over. We may not be able to determine when or if our partner will change, or when the pregnancy test will be positive, but we can acknowledge how we feel and turn our burdens over to God every time they intrude on our hearts and minds.

The second step is through acceptance. Acceptance transcends both resigned defeat and approval of unwelcome circumstances. We are simply accepting the realties in front of us while holding to the reality of faith—that God is caring for us every step of the way.

• ———— Day 1 Prompt: Acknowledging Reality ———— •

Radical acceptance simply means acknowledging reality. We might think the word *acceptance* means we're approving of or excusing painful circumstances or behavior, but acceptance is nothing of the sort. Acceptance brings peace because it helps us acknowledge reality as it's been and is. Fighting reality only leads to further suffering.

According to psychotherapist Sheri Van Dijk, acceptance doesn't mean waving a white flag in defeat. Rather, once we accept our current reality, we are better able to navigate it.[2] We can say, "This is happening or has happened. How do I want to handle it?" In other words, practicing acceptance leads to effective problem solving.

Acceptance also gives us a way out of cycles that keep us stuck. It took me years to understand this, but once I did, it changed everything. Acceptance is the choice to align ourselves with reality while keeping our hearts soft toward God's promises for a different and more hopeful reality.

Living It Out 🌿 Write down what feels most radical to you about accepting your current reality, and what has made it most difficult to do so.

----------- **Day 2 Prompt: Acceptance Releases Strength** -----------

Some of the most powerful words of acceptance were said by Jesus in the Garden of Gethsemane hours before his death. As he is there, wrestling with the reality of the Cross, he asks the Father if there is any other way to redeem humanity. And almost in the same breath, he utters these powerful words of acceptance: "Yet not my will, but yours be done" (Luke 22:42, NIV).

The moment Jesus uttered these words, Scripture says, "At once an angel from heaven was at his side, strengthening him" (verse 43, MSG). Acceptance not only brought peace but also strength. Acceptance released what Jesus needed so he could face the reality of the Cross.

Living It Out 🌿 Write down what you have been asking God to change or spare you from as it relates to your waiting. How can acceptance release what you need?

----------- **Day 3 Prompt: The Way to Peace** -----------

"In Acceptance Lieth Peace" by Amy Carmichael is one of my favorite poems. It beautifully speaks to our collective wrestling to find peace within circumstances we feel powerless to change.

IN ACCEPTANCE LIETH PEACE
He said, "I will accept the breaking sorrow
Which God to-morrow
Will to His son explain."
Then did the turmoil deep within him cease.

Not vain the word, not vain;
For in Acceptance lieth peace.[3]

Living It Out 🌿 Find and read the entire poem online. Write down how it relates to your experience of acceptance and waiting.

─── Day 4 Prompt: Trust While You Wait ───

The practice of identifying and focusing on what we *do* have control over helps us live wholeheartedly while we wait. One factor we can control is reaching out to someone we trust. We can FaceTime a family member, get coffee with a friend and share what's on our hearts, or simply be in the presence of someone we care about and who cares about us.

Reaching out in vulnerability is one of the wisest and most encouraging steps we can take while we wait.

Living It Out 🌿 Write down what you may need from your community today. Then reach out to someone you trust as a way to connect and focus on what you can control during this season.

The Value of Clinging

But today I have hope,
So if we are able to hold onto nothing else,
may it be hope in our hands and love in our chest.
ARIELLE ESTORIA

WHEN I VISITED ISRAEL, I was awestruck walking through historical sites from stories I had heard since I was a little girl. One place we toured was the field of Boaz. I had heard Ruth and Boaz's unlikely love story many times growing up.

Their story is told in the book of Ruth and begins with Naomi; her husband, Elimelek; and their two sons, Mahlon and Kilion, moving to Moab because of a famine in Bethlehem. Tragically, Elimelek dies, and a number of years later, Mahlon marries Ruth, and Kilion marries Orpah. Tragedy strikes again when Naomi's two sons die, leaving Ruth and Orpah widowed and Naomi without any blood relatives.

Naomi decides to return to Bethlehem and urges her daughters-in-law to go back to their families to start their lives over. "Return home, my daughters. Why would you come with me? Am I going to have any more sons, who could become your husbands?" (Ruth 1:11, NIV). We can hear the heartache in Naomi's voice. She has lost her whole family, and at this point in history, it was dangerous for a woman to be without a man to provide for her. Imagine her desperation as she picks up the shattered pieces and tries to start over.

Ruth and Orpah have two distinctly different responses. "Orpah kissed her mother-in-law goodbye, but Ruth *clung* to her" (Ruth 1:14, NIV, emphasis mine). *The Message* says, "Ruth embraced her and held on." In the midst of tragedy, Ruth clung to Naomi when there was no reason to.

Ruth made a radical, countercultural decision to hold on when it didn't make sense. She went against every fiber of reason and clung to what was precious to her.

When we ache from waiting, it makes sense to kiss our hopes goodbye—like Orpah kissed Naomi goodbye. We're tempted to part ways with our dreams and desires because it seems foolish to remain loyal to them.

What Ruth, Naomi, and Orpah never could have fathomed were the redemptive details up ahead. Ruth finds uncommon favor with Boaz, a wealthy bachelor who happens to be a kinsman redeemer—a male relative who can act on behalf of a relative in need.

Ruth marries Boaz, and their story brings restoration not only to their own lives but also to Naomi's. Ruth's choice to cling in the face of tragedy rather than kissing her hopes goodbye reminds us to hold on to God and his promises even when it appears foolish. What was true in Ruth's story is also true for ours—our clinging is not just for us. It's also for those around and ahead of us. Ruth's story teaches us that when it makes most sense to part ways with hope, it's most important to hold on.

Day 1 Prompt: Releasing and Clinging

As we wait, we need to discern what to cling to and what to release. It's tempting to think in terms of all-or-nothing—hold on to everything or let go of it all. But life is too complex for that.

For example, I often explain to clients that as children we clung to immature ways of protecting ourselves. But holding on to these behaviors as adults prevents us from meaningful connections with others. Growth and freedom are found in knowing when to cling and when to release. Ecclesiastes 3:5 says there is "a right time to hold on and another to let go" (MSG).

Living It Out 🌿 What have you let go of that you need to pick back up? And what are you clinging to that you need to release? Write down a list for both. Then choose one item from each to release and to pick back up.

Day 2 Prompt: The Place You and God Meet

God is barely mentioned in the book of Ruth, but he was active behind the scenes while everyday people were making extraordinary choices.

Psalm 77:19-20 says, "Your path led through the sea, your way through the mighty waters, though your footprints were not seen. You led your people like a flock by the hand of Moses and Aaron" (NIV).

This verse illustrates the intersection of sovereignty and humanity. God led the children of Israel through the Red Sea, although no one could discern his presence, while Moses and Aaron led the people into safety. When we cannot trace God in our waiting, he is still present. He is active behind the scenes and trusting *you* to make bold and brave choices.

Living It Out 🌿 What moment can you look back on and see God's involvement? How does it give you hope to believe that even though you cannot trace him now, he is still present? Write down what comes to mind.

Day 3 Prompt: Knowing Where to Go

The amount of grief and trauma in Ruth's story is shocking. In the span of ten years, Ruth's mother-in-law, Naomi, loses her husband and two sons, and she and Orpah lose their husbands. The name Naomi means "pleasant," so it's no wonder that when she returns to Bethlehem, she tells everyone to call her Mara, meaning "bitter."

How often has grief made us want to change our names so they no longer mean "pleasant" but "bitter"? If you have felt bitter toward God and your circumstances, it's okay. At some point, we all find ourselves there.

What was vital for Naomi, and for us too, is that she knew where to go. She went back to Bethlehem, which means "house of bread." She returned to a place that could nourish her broken heart.

Living It Out 🌿 Where is your "house of bread"? It could be a physical place, a person, or even the refuge you find in prayer. Write down what comes to mind.

Day 4 Prompt: Learning to Honor Yourself

There will be times when we make choices others don't understand. In these moments, we might refuse feedback or abandon our beliefs altogether.

Ruth made a radical choice to honor herself when she clung to Naomi and followed her to a foreign place. By honoring what was precious to her, she also honored Naomi and God. *This* is the hidden benefit of staying true to ourselves—we honor God and others in the process.

Remaining faithful to our convictions is a beautiful place of tension—a place where we are receptive to others' perspectives without the obligation to discard our own.

Living It Out 🌿 What decisions have been difficult to explain to those around you? How can the perspective from today's prompt help you honor yourself while remaining receptive to those you trust? Write down what comes to mind.

Time for a Change

My times are in your hands.

PSALM 31:15, NIV

WHEN SPRING WARMS THE EARTH, I look forward to taking my dog for walks. One of these afternoons was particularly beautiful. I felt the gentle breeze as birds sang and my dog searched for squirrels to chase. I smiled as I passed each home and took in the beauty of budding flowers. Nature seemed to whisper, "You can breathe now."

I realized how long I had been holding my breath. I exhaled and thought, *Spring is here.*

As I looked around, I saw the most stunning dogwood tree. Its white and pink blossoms were lovely, and it reminded me of how I feel at the ocean—I could gaze at it forever, and it still wouldn't be enough.

As I was taking in the whole tree, something made me laugh. A string of Christmas lights awkwardly hung from the bottom branches, looking out of place. The tree was the picture of spring but had remnants of winter clumsily draping over its branches. I thought how easy it is for an old season to cling to us when we are clearly entering a new one.

In my work with clients, I understand that everyone's experience is unique when it comes to their readiness to change. This understanding comes from the Transtheoretical model, which helps us appreciate the following stages of change: Precontemplation (*No*), Contemplation (*Maybe*), Preparation (*Prepare/Plan*), Action (*Do*), and Maintenance (*Keep Going*).[1]

I help my clients identify what stage they're in and support them as they move from one to the next. Discomfort is the common denominator in every stage. Change involves getting uncomfortable. Whenever we transition from the known to the unknown, we can expect discomfort.

I'm sure you have experienced disappointment and discouragement along the way. The longer you've waited, the more likely it is that disappointment and discouragement will have a chance to make a home in your heart.

With the arrival of spring, we're reminded to shake off the discouragement that has wrapped itself around our hearts. It's a seasonal permission slip to hope. Like those Christmas lights clinging to a tree that has transitioned to another season, reopening our hearts to hope can feel uncomfortable and out of place.

Choosing change and hope requires us to risk. These risks are important because the alternative is overstaying a season that's over.

> For everything there is a season, a time for every activity under heaven. . . . A time to plant and a time to harvest. . . . A time to tear down and a time to build up. A time to cry and a time to laugh. A time to grieve and a time to dance.
> ECCLESIASTES 3:1-4, NLT

It's important that we discern when it's time to take the uncomfortable risks and open our hearts to hopeful possibilities again.

•——— Day 1 Prompt: Learning from the Seasons ———•

According to Dr. Liz Carter, a naturopathic doctor, "in Chinese medicine, the seasons play an integral role in our lives and health. . . . The seasons are a huge part of how nature guides our internal temperament. When we really take a moment to feel the season with all our senses, we nourish ourselves. We align with the season and connect with a vital part of ourselves. The more we align our lives with the seasons, the more easily our lives will flow."[2]

God gave us the seasons as physical guides to align our lives with. Seasons create rhythm and order and remind us there is a time for everything.

Living It Out 🌿 Consider one aspect that only exists in the season of spring that speaks to what you need in *this* season of your waiting. Is it the hope you feel when you see a bud break forth? Is it the warmth of the air that causes your heart to soften and your spirit to lift? How can you align yourself with this season to hear God through what you can see, hear, smell, and touch? Write down what comes to mind.

Day 2 Prompt: "Look and Learn How to See"

In Matthew 24:32-33, Jesus says, "Now learn this lesson from the fig tree: As soon as its twigs get tender and its leaves come out, you know that summer is near. Even so, when you see all these things, you know that it is near, right at the door" (NIV).

In *Jesus' Plan for a New World: The Sermon on the Mount*, Richard Rohr says, "[God] most often uses *nature* as an authority. He points to clouds, sunsets, sparrows, lilies, corn in the field, leaves unfolding. . . . Nature instructs us everywhere. Look and learn how to see. Look and see the rhythm, the seasons, the life and death of things. That's your teaching, that's creation's plan in front of you."[3]

"Look and learn how to see." When I paused to take in the tree and noticed the lights, God was teaching me how to look and see. He is drawing you into similar moments.

Living It Out 🌱 How is God teaching you to look and see? Go for a walk this week and ask God to show you something in this spring season that can help you navigate your current season of waiting.

Day 3 Prompt: Moving with the Seasons

So often we choose to stay in uncomfortable places simply because they are familiar. The winter seasons of waiting are full of solitude, and although so much transformation happens there, it's not meant to last forever. We are meant to go from winter to spring, from barrenness to new life. When we believe that God has something amazing for us, we're willing to choose hope and risk disappointment. I have received so much good from choosing hope, and I have also survived moments of disappointment when situations didn't go as expected.

Staying close and connected to God gives us strength to transition with the seasons and maneuver through the unfamiliar. The nearness of the Holy Spirit comforts, encourages, and reminds us of who we are, no matter the outcome.

Living It Out 🌿 Write down what will help you bravely choose the unfamiliar and move into the spring season of your waiting.

——— Day 4 Prompt: One Close, True Friend ———

Waiting for fulfilled desires and answered prayers is lonely enough without adding changes and transitions to it.

Sociologist Dr. Marika Lindholm wrote an article called "Combatting the Loneliness of Transition" and offers the following advice:

> Combatting loneliness isn't just about being surrounded by lots of people; you will also need at least one close, true friend. "When a relationship lacks closeness, you'll sense that the other person doesn't really know you and/or doesn't really care about you," writes relationship coach Kira Asatryan. "Loneliness is essentially sadness caused by a lack of closeness. . . . One true friend can quell the loneliness of transition."[4]

Living It Out 🌿 If you have been feeling especially lonely because of the added pressure from recent transitions, identify one close, true friend you can confide in who can help "quell the loneliness of transition."

Trust God from the
bottom of your heart;
don't try to figure out
everything on your own.
Listen for God's voice
in everything you do,
everywhere you go.

Proverbs 3:5-6, MSG

SUMMER

FOR MANY OF US, summer evokes a symphony of nostalgic memories. When we were children, it might have looked like riding bikes with friends, sidewalk chalk, sleepovers with popcorn and movies, and nowhere to be the next day. In our teen years, it might have been the joy of being free from the constraints of school and driving around with friends while blasting music with the windows down. In our adulthood, summer still brings freedom as we step away from the demands of work to vacation and relax. Summer offers refreshment, awakening the joy often lost in the hustle and confinement of previous seasons.

Although summer may still be marked by waiting and carrying the daily weight of unfulfilled desires, childlike wonder reminds us anything is possible. In different seasons, hope might have felt like an illusion or a myth. But in summer, hope draws us close, bringing an overwhelming sense of relief. We see hidden opportunities within our waiting. Opportunities to learn and grow. We saw only shut doors in other seasons, but here we discern every "no" and "not yet" as opportunities to practice waiting with hope.

The famous poet William Carlos Williams says that "in summer the song sings itself."[5]

Summer has a lightness to it. It reminds us of the beauty of simplicity. Simplicity to believe that God is working in and through the details of our lives. Sustaining a hopeful melody requires less effort here, whereas in other seasons, we hummed our songs through grief and tears.

Our voices are amplified by the acoustics of the season, bringing an ease to our song. Hope feels within reach. There is a renewed youthfulness to our waiting, nudging us to live with a lighthearted spirit. Words in summer beckon us to rest and be refreshed by the hope-filled possibilities within and without us.

False Summits

*This mountain climbing [of life] is serious business, but glorious.
It takes strength and steady step to find the summits.*

L. B. COWMAN, *STREAMS IN THE DESERT*

IT WAS JANUARY 2020, and I was beside myself. I went into 2019 with high hopes for all that would change before the year ended, only to reach the top of a new year the same.

I sat across from a friend at a coffee shop, trying to cover up the raw emotion I was feeling. Although anger oozed out as I talked, I knew underneath was deep disappointment.

An "Anger Iceburg" is a picture I reference with clients when talking about emotions. Similar to an actual iceburg, only 10 percent of our emotions sit on the surface where we can see them, and the other 90 percent live below our conscious awareness. We're quick to recognize anger and frustration because generally they feel less tender to express. But feelings such as sadness, hurt, or disappointment are more vulnerable, so we keep them hidden.

Back in the coffee shop, an unexpected picture began to emerge. For a long time, I felt like I was climbing a steep mountain in hopes of reaching the "top." Meaning, prayers would finally be answered and long-awaited desires would be fulfilled. But instead, I reached some other top *below* the top.

"Oh, you reached the false summit," my friend said.

I looked at her, surprised. "What do you mean? What's a false summit?"

She explained how a false summit is a peak that appears to be the pinnacle of a mountain, but as you get closer, it turns out the real summit is actually farther up.

I couldn't believe how perfectly this language described how I felt.

In mountaineering, a false peak can have significant discouraging effects on climbers' psychological states by inducing feelings of lost hope and even failure.

Before this conversation with my friend, God had given me the word *discipline,* and it wasn't until this moment that I understood why.

Hebrews 12:11 says, "All discipline seems to be painful at the time, yet later it will produce a transformation of character, bringing a harvest of righteousness and peace to those who yield to it."

I reached a false summit in my waiting, and all the proverbial climbing I had done in other seasons had left me emotionally and physically depleted. The discipline required to rest, recover, and keep moving forward felt impossible, but I believed God would develop it in me as I continued my journey.

Maybe you've reached your own false summit, and you feel depleted and hopeless. Pain may be the means by which we arrive at our actual summits, but joy—deep fulfilling joy—is always the goal.

The joy set before Jesus strengthened him to endure the Cross (Hebrews 12:2), and it's joy that empowers us to step boldly into this day, month, and year. When we feel tired and hopeless, joy is hard to find, but it's what we need most. If you're looking for joy in your circumstances, you may not find it. But if you're looking for joy in God, you will always find it. This joy will strengthen you to keep putting one foot in front of the other.

•——————— **Day 1 Prompt: Exploring below the Surface** ———————•

The "Anger Iceberg" was developed by the Gottman Institute, led by psychologist John Gottman. One of their team members, Kyle Benson, says, "When we're angry, there can be other emotions hidden beneath the surface. It's easy to see a person's anger, but it can be difficult to see the underlying feelings the anger is protecting."

Anger is a purposeful emotion. It alerts us to unjust situations and shields us from other emotions that seem scary or make us feel more vulnerable. The article goes on to say, "There are times when other emotions are spurring the anger and we use anger to protect the raw feelings that lie beneath it."[1]

Living It Out 🌿 What emotions have been lurking underneath anger? In your journal, draw an iceberg with 10 percent above the surface and the remaining 90 percent below the surface. In the 10 percent space, write emotions you are aware of. And in the larger (90 percent) space below, write emotions your anger is protecting you from feeling.

————— Day 2 Prompt: Training, *not* Punishment —————

Can you imagine the sheer panic of watching a small child run across a busy street? Chills would shoot up your spine as you run to shield her from harm. Once the child is safe, her parents would lovingly but firmly correct her and explain the danger.

Hebrews 12:7 says, "It's the child [God] loves that he disciplines; the child he embraces, he also corrects. . . . This trouble you're in isn't punishment; it's *training*, the normal experience of children. Only irresponsible parents leave children to fend for themselves" (MSG).

The discipline God develops in us is training, not punishment. It creates the resilience to wait well and prepares us for all God intends to give.

Living It Out 🌿 Has waiting felt like punishment rather than God's loving discipline? How could Hebrews 12:7 and the example of parents lovingly disciplining their child reveal something new about how God is working in your waiting? Write down what comes to mind.

————— Day 3 Prompt: Joy Gives Way to Hope —————

Writer and theologian C. S. Lewis wrote *Surprised by Joy.* A former atheist, Lewis said what surprised him most after putting his faith in Christ was joy; hence the title of his book. He wrote, "All Joy reminds. It is never a possession, always a desire for something longer ago or further away or still 'about to be.'"[2]

This speaks to the meaningful relationship between joy and hope as we wait. Deep and fulfilling joy gives us strength to keep waiting with hope, the desire for something about to be. Hope softens our heart to joy, and joy strengthens our heart for hope.

Living It Out ❧ When have you been surprised by joy during your waiting? How did that joy-filled moment give way to hope? Reflect and write down the memories and thoughts that come to mind.

Day 4 Prompt: Unconditional Positive Regard

My friend who sat with me as I poured out my anger is the perfect example of someone who has journeyed through her own pain and learned to create a space for someone else to do the same.

She didn't judge my angry feelings. Rather, she saw the tender feelings beneath them. She demonstrated something called *unconditional positive regard*, which is "support and acceptance of a person no matter what that person says or does."[3] It is a valuable gift I offer my clients, and being on the receiving end of it that day reminded me how important it is.

Living It Out ❧ How can you show unconditional positive regard to someone in your world today—by praying for someone also navigating a difficult season? Whatever it is, make a plan to practice unconditional positive regard.

Growing in Flexibility

Between stimulus and response there is a space. In that space is our power to choose our response. In our response lies our growth and our freedom.[1]

ATTRIBUTED TO VIKTOR E. FRANKL

I LOVE YOGA, although I'm not naturally flexible. (I had to work pretty hard to touch my toes, if that gives you an indication of what I'm working with.) At a recent class, the instructor set an intention to focus on but did so by talking about the discomfort of waiting. She explained how in yoga, as is in life, when we move quickly through the poses, we escape the discomfort of them. Whereas when we challenge our bodies and minds to *wait* in the pose, we feel a rush of uncomfortable sensations.

"Flexibility doesn't come from working, it comes from waiting," she said, as she invited us to step into each pose and wait to feel the discomfort and tension that met us when we didn't rush into the next move.

Pushing and striving into flexibility may give us a sense of control and a way out of unpleasant emotions, but we forfeit valuable benefits in the process.

I hadn't realized the interdependent relationship between flexibility and waiting. Waiting challenges us to grow in flexibility, and increased flexibility empowers us to wait differently. No wonder there are so many Bible verses about patient endurance and waiting. Perhaps God wants us to know that flexibility grows while we wait, and flexibility develops resilience to wait with hope.

Even in times of trouble we have a joyful confidence, knowing that our pressures will develop in us patient endurance. And patient endurance will refine our character, and proven character leads us back to hope.

ROMANS 5:3-4

"Pressures will develop." I love that. We often associate waiting with inactivity or passivity, but so much is developed in us and on our behalf while we wait.

The pressure is developing flexibility in you. It's refining your character and leading you back to hope. In other words, it is enabling you to wait from a transformed place. The transformation isn't glamorous. It's often slow and painful. But with every choice to slow down and relax into the discomfort, you are growing in patience, flexibility, and surrender.

──────── Day 1 Prompt: The Relationship between ────────
Waiting and Flexibility

The understanding that flexibility comes from waiting rather than working was revolutionary to me. After that yoga session, I wasn't surprised to find research that confirmed this concept.

According to professional athletes and trainers, there is an optimal way to stretch and gain flexibility. "Gradually and carefully move your body or the limb being stretched into the stretch position. Once you feel slight tension in the muscle, hold the position. . . . Wait 15 seconds and then stretch further. After approximately 15 seconds, your body's natural stretch inhibiting reflex will relax, allowing you to stretch a little more. Gently ease a little further into the stretch and hold for a further 15 seconds."[2]

Our bodies are designed to gain flexibility by waiting, and our minds and hearts aren't any different. When we're confronted by delays and unmet expectations and we choose to wait, we grow in flexibility that empowers us to wait from a place of rest and peace.

Living It Out 🌿 Take a yoga class or stretch at home this week with this principle of waiting in mind. Notice the sensations that come up while you wait in each pose. Journal what you notice.

Day 2 Prompt: Uncharted Territory

It's important to have a guide when you're navigating uncharted territory. When you visit a national park, a guide shows you the highlights. When you go to a workout class, an instructor guides you through the moves. When you tour a historical site, a guide walks you through the authorized areas.

When we're waiting, we are traversing unexplored territory in our lives and within ourselves. Through countless unknowns, we need a guide who provides encouragement to keep going. It's helpful in a yoga class when the instructor does the poses with us. It feels less lonely to have someone experiencing the discomfort too. Jesus is the best guide we could ask for because he took on human flesh, identifying with our humanity. He was our guide then and now.

Living It Out 🌿 Read Hebrews 4:15 in *The Message*, and imagine God as a guide. Imagine him present to speak, adjust, encourage, and model how to wait. How does this change how you approach and feel about your waiting? Write down what you notice.

Day 3 Prompt: A Change of Pace

Within this idea of waiting and flexibility is the need to change our pace. The yoga teacher instructed us to pause in the pose rather than switch quickly into the next movement.

Generally, we have a difficult time slowing down. We move fast through life to avoid pain and discomfort but burn ourselves out in the process. We try to work our way into flexibility and end up injured and exhausted.

I can hear Jesus asking these questions: "Are you tired? Worn out? Burned out on religion? Come to me. Get away with me and you'll recover your life. I'll show you how to take a real rest. Walk with me and work with me—watch how I do it. Learn the unforced rhythms of grace. I won't lay anything heavy or ill-fitting on you. Keep company with me and you'll learn to live freely and lightly" (Matthew 11:28-30, MSG).

Living It Out 🌿 Consider how you have been trying to work your way into flexibility as you wait. Write down what the "unforced rhythms of grace" mean to you and what it might look like to incorporate this perspective into your life.

Day 4 Prompt: Refusing to Compare

If you have ever done a workout class then you know we not only need the instructor but also the encouragement from those doing the class alongside us. Although everyone possesses different skill levels, we are all learning and being challenged together.

If we're not careful, waiting can be a breeding ground for comparison, since others may have what you are still waiting for. What if instead of looking at each other and comparing ourselves, we aimed to learn about the strength others have gained as they navigated their hard moments? What if we learned about what has helped them? What if we refused to assume that others' lives are easier because they have what we desire? What if we remembered that no one has it easy, and all of us have overcome hardships many people will never know about?

Living It Out 🌿 Next time you're with a friend, ask about a difficult waiting moment in their life, what helped them through it, and the greatest lesson they learned because of it.

Root Causes

God, our God, will take care of the hidden things
but the revealed things are our business.
DEUTERONOMY 29:29, MSG

IT WAS A TYPICAL DAY as I stood in line at a local store, anxiously waiting to rush the cash register. Pressed for time, I was antsy while the customer in front of me paid.

Ugh, I hate waiting. It wasn't the first time I had this thought, but this time I caught myself. Awareness of my impatience sent me down such a deep train of thought I didn't see the cashier waving me to check out. I paid for my items and left, still preoccupied over where my thoughts had taken me.

It's normal to feel anxious when we're waiting. Whether it's in line at a store, or more seriously when we're waiting for a relationship to be mended or our career to take shape, we feel anxious and don't always know why.

I've had countless anxious moments waiting for circumstances to change. But eventually I became irritated with myself for not being able to shake the anxiety. When I talked with my therapist about this push and pull between anxiety and annoyance with myself, I had an unpleasant epiphany.

"I think I'm anxious because I feel entitled," I said, flashing an embarrassed expression. My therapist's emphatic "Wow" prompted nervous laughter from me because I knew it was true.

Growing up an only child was certainly a contributing factor. My parents grew up with little and wanted me to have everything they didn't. The subtle but powerful downside was that, more often than not, I got what I wanted, when I wanted it.

This dynamic shielded me from wrestling with the discomfort of not having life on my terms. The anxiety I felt as an adult was connected to the childish belief that I deserved what I wanted, when I wanted it. (You can see now why this was so uncomfortable to admit.)

Reparenting is a concept in psychology in which a therapist models a healthy relationship as a means to create powerful healing moments for their client.[1] Reparenting also happens through relationship with God, mentors, a spouse, friends, and even ourselves as healthy adults.

No one's upbringing was perfect, and all of us experienced some level of dysfunction that is perpetuated in our adult lives. Reparenting allows us to create corrective experiences for our younger and adult selves. For example, if we experienced a lack of structure, neglect, or invalidation as children, we can connect with our younger selves now to offer the validation and care that was missing then.

Part of the purpose behind my prolonged season of waiting was to allow God vital opportunities to reparent me. He was teaching me how to navigate the discomfort of not having life on my terms and uprooting entitlement that was keeping me anxious. The summer seasons of our waiting are often opportunities for God to grow us into greater emotional and spiritual health. "And patient endurance will refine our character, and proven character leads us back to hope" (Romans 5:3).

Your story is most likely different from mine. But I encourage you to consider whether there is any hidden entitlement in your heart. It's a mark of maturity to relinquish entitlement while also holding on to the belief that we are infinitely valuable to God, and he delights to give us the very best life has to offer.

Day 1 Prompt: A Hundred More Feet

My clinical supervisor used to say that recovery looks like spending less time *there*, and doing less harm *there*. This description speaks to the importance of taking manageable steps toward change to help ensure the change is long-lasting.

Anxiety disrupts our peace, and as we explore the underlying reasons, we need effective ways to manage it (i.e., "How can we spend less time there, and do less harm there?").

When there is a gap between where we are and where we want to be, we can ask ourselves, *What is a hundred feet farther from where I am?* Perhaps it's being curious rather than judgmental toward yourself. Maybe it's sharing about your anxiety with a trusted friend and allowing yourself to be seen.

Living It Out 🌿 Write down what "a hundred feet farther" from where you are looks like, and put those steps into action.

Day 2 Prompt: God as Both Mother and Father

Perhaps unmet needs while growing up left you ill-equipped for the difficulty of waiting. Children need to learn six vital life skills to be equipped for life's inevitable challenges: love and respect, self-belief and self-confidence, emotional management, and good communication skills.[2] If there was a deficiency in any of these, we may find waiting impossible and the resulting anxiety debilitating.

God wants to come alongside you as a good parent and provide what you need, not only so you can wait differently but also so you can *be* different.

Living It Out 🌿 Close your eyes and invite God, as a kind parent, into the part of waiting that feels most difficult for you right now. Notice how God approaches you with compassion to relieve your heart of anxiety. When you're ready, write down what you noticed.

Day 3 Prompt: Exploring the Root Cause of Our Anxiety

Feeling afraid is a normal part of being human. It's when fear evolves into anxiety that it indicates something deeper is going on. Chip Dodd, author of *The Voice of the Heart: A Call to Full Living*, explains how each primary emotion has a corresponding gift and impairment.[3] Anxiety is the impaired version of fear that has taken root, and consequently, taken on a life of its own.

My hidden entitlement followed this progression: "I am entitled to what I want, and if I don't get it, I feel afraid, angry, and disappointed." These emotions manifested in anxiety, making life feel hard. What belief is at the root of your anxiety?

Perhaps yours sounds like this: "I have *no control over what happens in my life,* and I feel *afraid, panicked, and angry.* These emotions manifest in anxiety, making *life feel unpredictable.*"

Living It Out ❧ Discovering the Root Cause:

I believe _____, and I feel
_____. These emotions manifest in anxiety,
making me feel _____.

Reframing with the Truth:

I believe I have authority as I partner with God in my life. When
I feel scared, I will open my heart for God to love and comfort me
through the difficult moments.

—————— **Day 4 Prompt: Turning the Lights On** ——————

First John 4:18 says, "There is no fear in love. But perfect love drives out fear, because fear has to do with punishment" (NIV).

This verse is like flipping on the light switch in a dark room. Fear is dark and confusing, but love is bright and clarifying. As we turn ourselves and our anxiety over to being loved by God and others, we are turning toward the light that dispels darkness.

Living It Out ❧ Think of someone with whom you can share about fearful narratives you have been rehearsing, and notice how this act of vulnerability brings light and clarity to your season of waiting.

Learning to Dance with Uncertainty

There is no form of self-expression that makes us feel more vulnerable than dancing. It's literally full-body vulnerability..

BRENÉ BROWN, *THE GIFTS OF IMPERFECTION*

HAVE YOU EVER SEEN SOMEONE who just cannot dance? Maybe at a wedding or a Zumba class at the gym? I once went to a Zumba class in Chicago with my friend Hannah. We almost passed out from stifling our laughter because the guy in front of us sincerely tried to do the moves but failed miserably.

This is how I feel trying to "dance" with uncertainty. I look like that rhythm-challenged guy desperately trying to move his hips to the music.

My friend Tara is an amazing dancer, and she explained that in order to dance with ease and rhythm, you need to face your fears of what others think and learn to feel comfortable in your body.

The process of learning to dance with uncertainty is not much different. We need to get comfortable being present with ourselves and learn to manage our fears differently.

When waiting triggered uncomfortable uncertainty, I managed my fears by managing the people or situations creating the uncertainty, rather than managing myself. It took time to relearn to regulate the fear that belonged to no one but me. Inadvertently, I stepped on a few toes in the process.

"Stepping on toes" can take on a few different forms. It can be pushing others to resolve situations when they aren't ready, or avoiding situations that require our attention, or manipulating others to get what we want.

Richard Rohr says, "Let the bared soul recall what it knows beneath its fear of the dark." My primary issue wasn't with uncertainty; it was with my fear of the dark. Uncertainty made my life look and feel dark, and darkness triggered fear in me. Rohr adds, "Not knowing or uncertainty is a kind of darkness that many people find unbearable."[1]

Uncertainty was unbearable because I was afraid of the dark, making it impossible to *dance* with it. I needed God's light to illuminate those dark places and impart courage to navigate the waiting moments.

In John 8:12 Jesus says, "I am the world's Light. No one who follows me stumbles around in the darkness. I provide plenty of light to live in" (MSG).

If you feel scared and clumsy trying to dance with uncertainty, Jesus "provide[s] plenty of light to live in." His love is like flipping on the switch in a dark room—it swallows our fear of darkness and gives us courage to face waiting and uncertainty with strength and sure-footedness.

———— Day 1 Prompt: Remembering What Is True ————

When I was a little girl I was terrified of the dark. My mom asked one of our pastors to record a prayer on cassette tape (Remember those?) that I could listen to every night before bed.

The pastor's soothing voice reminded me that angels stood by my doorway keeping me safe, and God's loving presence watched over me as I slept. With these visuals in mind, I felt fear release from my little body as I drifted off to sleep.

My fear of the dark lost its power when I remembered what was true—God loved me and was present to protect me. When we're faced with uncertainty, we regress to feeling like children who are scared of the dark. The remedy that worked then is the same that will work now—remembering God loves us and is present to protect us.

Living It Out 🌿 Write down a prayer to help you remember that God loves you and is present to protect you. Record this prayer on your phone or ask someone you trust to record it for you. Every time you feel fear's grip, play this recording to remind yourself what is true.

Day 2 Prompt: Being Present

Being present has given me more tolerance for uncertainty. It's easy to dwell in the past and forecast the future and miss the good happening now. In Exodus 3:14, when God speaks to Moses about going back to Egypt, he says, "You shall say this to the Israelites, 'I AM has sent me to you'" (AMP). God refers to himself as "I AM" because that is where he meets us—in the here and now.

Psalm 46:1 says, "God is our refuge and strength, an ever-present help in trouble" (NIV). As we meet God in this moment, we find strength to maneuver through the darkness of uncertainty.

Living It Out 🌿 What helps you be present with God? Going on a walk? Journaling, reading, praying, breathing, moving your body? Today, do whatever helps you center yourself in the moment with God.

Day 3 Prompt: The Freedom of Responsibility

One of the critical realizations I had was about taking responsibility for my emotions. Rather than managing my fear by managing everything around me, I learned to bravely face my fear of the dark.

Responsibility isn't glamourous, but it is liberating when we embrace it. Waiting brings up many unpleasant emotions, leaving us feeling victimized by circumstances outside our control.

But God hasn't called us to be victims. "The LORD will make you the head, not the tail. . . . You will always be at the top, never at the bottom" (Deuteronomy 28:13, NIV). God flips the paradigm and invites us to join him as victors.

Living It Out 🌿 What does it mean for you to be the head and not the tail, at the top and never the bottom? Does it mean you start believing differently? Talking to yourself more compassionately? Evaluating behaviors that may be reinforcing a victim mentality? Write down what comes to mind.

Day 4 Prompt: Shaking Off the Heaviness

When was the last time you had a spontaneous dance party? Growing up I had them all the time. One night in college my girlfriends and I went to one of our apartments, plugged in our iPods (showing my age here), blasted the volume, and literally danced the night away. We were a sweaty, happy mess at the end of it.

The older we get, the more vulnerable dancing feels. We forfeit freedom and joy when we're preoccupied with decorum and let fear take center stage. David danced before the Lord in 2 Samuel 6:14, and even when his wife Michal was offended at his liberated display, he didn't let it stifle his moment with God. Waiting makes life heavy, and it's important to be intentional about bringing lightness and joy to our lives whenever we can. And a dance party of one or a few is sometimes just what we need.

Living It Out 🌿 Find a time when you can blast the music and have a dance party by yourself at your house or with friends or family members. Let the heaviness fall off as you give in to joy and freedom.

Even in times of
trouble we have a joyful
confidence, knowing that
our pressures will develop
in us patient endurance.
And patient endurance will
refine our character, and
proven character leads us
back to hope.

Romans 5:3-4

When the Math Doesn't Check Out

Our answers will come. Our guidance will come.
Pray. Trust. Wait. Let go. We are being led. We are being guided.
MELODY BEATTIE, *THE LANGUAGE OF LETTING GO*

THE VIRTUE OF FAITH calculates very differently than logic or reason. The math involved in matters of faith doesn't exactly "check out" when we observe it from a human standpoint.

In Judges 6, we read about Gideon, whose tribe is oppressed by Midianites. "The angel of the LORD" (verse 12, NIV) approaches Gideon and commissions him to "save Israel out of Midian's hand" (verse 14, NIV). Gideon, full of fear and doubt, asks God for three miraculous signs to confirm that God's word can be trusted. After God fulfills Gideon's requests and his army of thirty-two thousand readies for battle, something unusual happens.

> The LORD said to Gideon, "You have too many warriors with you.
> If I let all of you fight the Midianites, the Israelites will boast to me
> that they saved themselves by their own strength. Therefore, tell
> the people, 'Whoever is timid or afraid may leave this mountain
> and go home.'"
> JUDGES 7:2-3, NLT

Twenty-two thousand went home, leaving only ten thousand to fight. According to God's calculations, that was still too many. He tells Gideon that the men who cup their hands to drink from the spring are the ones to fight. As a result, Gideon sends 9,700 more men home and faces the fiercest battle of his life with *three hundred men*. Can you imagine? Gideon finally gathers courage, only for God to whittle his army to a meager three hundred men.

Talk about the math not checking out.

Knowing Gideon's fear, God leads him to the Midianite camp, where he overhears enemy soldiers talking about a dream that prophesied an Israelite victory.

With this boost of confidence, Gideon instructs his army to follow his lead and blow their horns after he and his companions do. Then they were to shout, "For the LORD and for Gideon!" (7:17-18, NLT). When Gideon's army does this, "the LORD caused the warriors in the camp to fight against each other with their swords" (7:22, NLT). Whoever remained fled in different directions.

Prior to this battle, God had fulfilled Gideon's three requests for signs, knowing the faith he would later require of Gideon. God first meets him on the mathematical grounds Gideon understands and then asks Gideon to trust the calculations of faith.

In the summer seasons of waiting, God invites us to believe him in ways that don't fit our human calculations. And like Gideon, we ask for confirmations we understand so we can eventually meet God on the unfamiliar grounds of faith he's inviting us to.

Hebrews 11:3 says, "By faith we understand" (NIV). Faith can only be understood when we live and move in trust. Outside of faith, so much of what God asks of us doesn't make sense. In other words, the math won't check out.

God graciously meets us where we are before he beckons us to meet him where he is. Romans 1:17 says, "For in it the righteousness of God is revealed from faith to faith; as it is written, 'The just shall live by faith'" (NKJV).

As God meets us on grounds we can grasp and we accept the invitation to meet him on his, our faith deepens, allowing us to partner with him in ways that seem impossible but always check out in the end.

— Day 1 Prompt: A Wise Mind —

With clients, I often draw a diagram called "The Wise Mind." This diagram illustrates the relationship between the logical and emotional sides of our minds.

I draw two circles that partly overlap, like a Venn diagram. One is marked *logic* and the other *emotion*. If we tend to be more logical, we lean more on the circle to the left, and if we are more emotional, we may lean more into the circle to the right.

The middle space integrates logic and emotion, and inside it I write the word *wisdom*. When faith's calculations contest our logic and emotion, this integrated place empowers us to engage these challenges with wisdom.

Living It Out 🌿 Find "The Wise Mind" diagram online. In your journal, draw your own version as you reflect on James 1:5: "If you need wisdom, ask our generous God, and he will give it to you" (NLT). Write down which aspects of wisdom you currently need from God.

Day 2 Prompt: The Promise of His Presence

When God first speaks to Gideon, he says, "The Lord is with you, you mighty man of [fearless] courage" (Judges 6:12, AMPC). Gideon replies, "If the LORD is with us, then why has all this happened to us? . . . But now the LORD has abandoned us and put us into the hand of Midian" (Judges 6:13, AMP).

God affirms his presence and Gideon's identity. He essentially says, "You aren't alone, and I believe in you." You can hear Gideon's pain when he expresses how abandoned he feels. You may relate to this sentiment. When we feel abandoned in the wait, God's promise to us is "You aren't alone, and I believe in you."

Living It Out 🌿 How do the words *You aren't alone, and I believe in you* land for you as you move through seasons of waiting? Are they comforting, relieving, or difficult to believe? Write down how you experience these words from God today.

Day 3 Prompt: Calculating with God in View

The story of the walls of Jericho in Joshua 6 is another instance where the math doesn't check out. Well before anything happens, God declares to Joshua that he has delivered Jericho into his hands. This was an outlandish statement since the walls of Jericho were impenetrable by any human calculation. Additionally, God's strategy is even more unusual. God instructs them to march around the wall for seven days before they blast their trumpets and shout.

In his devotional *My Utmost for His Highest*, Oswald Chambers says, "God seems to have a delightful way of upsetting the things we have calculated on without taking Him into account."[1] As we're waiting and walking in faith, we are also learning to submit our human calculations to God and calculate with him in view.

Living It Out 🌿 What difficult waiting moments have challenged you to calculate with God in view? Write down what comes to mind.

Day 4 Prompt: A Helpful Reminder

It's invaluable to surround ourselves with people who remind us of who we are when the pain of waiting causes us to forget. In the same way God approached Gideon and affirmed his identity, we can affirm each other.

When we doubt and forget who we are, trusted community can refresh our memories. Morgan Harper Nichols says, "You are who you are: a living, breathing human being who has a soul in need of Truth and Grace to make it through these things."[2]

Living It Out 🌿 Reflect on this quote and consider when someone has reminded you who you are. Think about opportunities you have to extend this same gift to others.

Mender of Broken Hearts

He heals the brokenhearted and binds up their wounds.

PSALM 147:3, ESV

IN 2005, I lost the man I loved in a car accident. Our story was beautiful and in some ways tragic. I remember wondering how the sun was still shining and the earth was still turning when my whole world had stopped.

Shattered. The feeling was new to me then, but now I can recognize it as grief. Picking up the pieces to repair my broken heart felt impossible. A part of me wasn't sure I wanted to, which was another strange sensation, but one I now understand as well.

When we lose someone, we're afraid to move away from the pain because it feels like the only thing still connecting us. We think if we start to enjoy life again, the memory of our loved one will slip through our fingers a little more.

After his funeral, my friend Liz drove me back to my house and said, "Just focus on right now. Brush your teeth, wash your face, and get some rest. And then do the same thing tomorrow. Take it minute by minute, as hard as it is, and don't think too far ahead."

So every morning I would wake up with a broken heart and choose to put one foot in front of the other.

The marathon exhaustion of waiting for a broken heart to heal is among life's most painful experiences. Healing the complexity of our hearts does not happen on our timetable. Even two years after that loss, I woke up with heaviness and muddled through my days, longing for someone who was no longer there.

I needed God to do something, to miraculously restore me, but I didn't even know how to ask for that.

Then one cold night in February, I was once again sitting in Liz's car, crying while I told her I could no longer take this longing.

She listened and said, "Okay, let's pray then. Let's pray for God to heal your heart."

I felt a glimmer of hope and agreed. She asked God to put the pieces back together and then hugged me, and I went home that night a little more hopeful.

Winter turned into spring, which turned into summer, and one morning I woke up early. I dragged myself to the shower, not thinking much of anything.

The spray of warm water brought my tired mind and body to life, and it dawned on me that my heart didn't feel as broken. I stood there, stunned. It was as if God had performed surgery on my heart as I slept. It was sore but no longer broken. The tightness, pain, and heaviness had subsided.

And the longing to be with a man who was no longer there? That had subsided too. I wept tears of joy as I realized my season of waiting for God to heal my heart had ended.

My grief certainly didn't end there—that's not how grief works. But God took away the debilitating pain so I could breathe and open my heart to someday love again.

You aren't alone in your wait to feel whole again and the desire for a new chapter. God is not only near to those with a broken heart but also the Mender of broken hearts.

Keep bringing your grief to him. He intends to heal and release your heart.

•——————— Day 1 Prompt: Caring for Our Bodies ———————•

Grief can be a physical ache as much as an emotional one. Studies reveal the powerful effects grief can have on the body, including increased inflammation, a weakened immune system, increased blood pressure, and "broken heart syndrome."[1]

A Harvard Health article explains how this syndrome is a direct response to severe emotional and physical stress, including grief. It's believed that the surge of adrenaline released during stress and grief "stuns" the heart, making it feel broken.² Grief is a physical pain, and we need to care for our bodies and minds.

Living It Out 🌿 Full-body breathing is one way we can find relief from the grief we hold in our bodies. Close your eyes, and put your right hand on your heart and your left hand on your stomach. Take deep, slow breaths in through your nose; then with each exhale, focus on a different area: forehead, jaw, shoulders, chest, belly. Continue through your hips, legs, and feet. Notice what feels different.

Day 2 Prompt: When Pain Feels Problematic

Prolonged pain takes its toll mentally and physically. At one point I believed emotional pain meant something must be wrong and needed to be remedied immediately. But not all pain is a result of dysfunction. Some pain is a necessary response to something that matters to us, and if we face it and feel it, we can grow and deepen in new ways.

In *The Problem of Pain*, C. S. Lewis says, "We can ignore even pleasure. But pain insists upon being attended to. God whispers to us in our pleasures, speaks in our conscience, but shouts in our pains: it is His megaphone to rouse a deaf world."³

I don't subscribe to the idea that God engineers or inflicts pain, but I absolutely believe he uses it for his purposes and his glory in our lives. Even in this place you would rather not be, God wants to speak to you, change you, and heal you.

Living It Out 🌿 Listen to the song "Mended" by Watermark. Allow the lyrics and melody to speak to you about how God wants to come close to mend the hurting places in your heart.

Day 3 Prompt: When Pain Makes Itself at Home

As much as pain feels problematic, we can become accustomed to living with it. It can wrap itself around our identity, making it difficult to know who we would be without it. This reality is often difficult to recognize because it conflicts with our desire for the pain to go away.

Psalm 139:23 says, "God, I invite your searching gaze into my heart. Examine me through and through; find out everything that may be hidden within me. "

Sometimes God waits to take away the pain until we're ready to give it to him.

Living It Out  Reflect and ask yourself if letting go of the pain of waiting has been more difficult than you realized. Allow God to search your heart and show you whether pain has made a home in your heart. Ask him to give you courage to release it into his care.

Day 4 Prompt: Doing the Next Right Thing

My friend Liz encouraged me to do the next right thing and release any pressure to think beyond the present moment. She listened and prayed for me when I didn't have strength or words. We need to remind each other to take each season one moment at a time and to pray for one another along the way.

Living It Out Who is waiting through a season of grief and may need you to extend this kindness? Reflect, and write down who comes to mind. Reach out to them in some way this week.

An Active Participant

All good things are worth waiting for and worth fighting for.
ATTRIBUTED TO SUSAN GALE

WAITING FEELS MORE PAINFUL if we believe we are supposed to be passive in the process. I see this idea play out in relationships, particularly in dating. Societal norms and the theology we adhere to shape our beliefs about how men and women "should" interact.

Without taking a broad stroke to a complex topic, I think it's fair to say that within Christendom there are strong ideologies that pigeonhole men as the active pursuer and women as the passive responder.

There is certainly intention behind how God created men and women and the uniqueness each brings to a relationship. However, excessive emphasis on men as the sole pursuer and initiator often leaves women feeling it would be inappropriate to reciprocate these roles.

The Gottman Institute's research on marriage and family found that "when a man is not willing to share power with his partner, there is an 81% chance that his marriage will self-destruct."[1] This noteworthy statistic communicates the need for both parties to maintain their agency for a healthy relationship to exist.

Especially as women, imbalanced perspectives can impact how we think we are "supposed" to interact with God. We end up holding misguided beliefs that God holds all the power and we hold none. This idea contradicts the principles of faith in Scripture.

Luke 17:6 says, "You don't need *more* faith. There is no 'more' or 'less' in faith. If you have a bare kernel of faith . . . you could say to this sycamore tree, 'Go jump in the lake,' and it would do it" (MSG).

Mark 11:23 says, "If anyone says to this mountain, 'Go, throw yourself into the sea,' and does not doubt in their heart but believes that what they say will happen, it will be done for them" (NIV).

Jesus intentionally taught his disciples about how powerful their faith was. Although they were never meant to do his part, he certainly empowered them to do theirs.

Another example of this active partnership is in Genesis 32:9, 12: "O God of my father Abraham . . . *you who said to me,* 'Go back to your country and your relatives, and I will make you prosper'. . . *you have said,* 'I will surely make you prosper and will make your descendants like the sand of the sea'" (NIV, emphasis mine).

Streams in the Desert author, L. B. Cowman, says, "[Jacob] began by quoting God's promise: 'Thou saidst.' He did so twice (9 and 12). Ah, he has got God in his power then! God puts Himself within our reach in His promises."[2]

God puts himself within our reach. This is a vital perspective in our waiting. God is not distant, aloof, or unapproachable. He is accessible, engaged, and empowering. We are not meant to assume the posture of a passive responder, but rather an empowered participant in God's plan unfolding in our lives.

•——————— Day 1 Prompt: The Language of Shame ———————•

Whenever I hear my client repeat the word *should*, I gently bring it to their attention. "Shoulds" are the language of shame. "I should do that. I shouldn't have done that." They are tied up in obligation and self-criticism—which adds more fuel to shame's fire.

When we observe ourselves using the word *should*, we need to evaluate whether shame is the driving force. Shoulds make waiting more difficult, and they perpetuate shame and keep us from connection with God and others. Words such as *can* or *get to* connote agency and open our hearts to self-compassion. The language we use reflects so much of what is going on inside our hearts.

Living It Out 🌿 Have you found yourself using the word *should*? What does this word represent to you, and how can swapping out *should* for *can* or *get to* lift your heart out of shame? Write down what comes to mind.

• ——————— **Day 2 Prompt: You Matter to God** ——————— •

It's mind-boggling that the God of the universe makes promises to us. King David wrote, "What is mankind that you are mindful of them, human beings that you care for them?" (Psalm 8:4, NIV).

A promise from God is more than a pact; it's a covenant that reveals God's desire to be in relationship with us. It reflects our value to him. Psalm 17:8 says we are the "apple of [his] eye" (NIV). If you have something stuck in your eye or someone pokes you in the eye, you know how disorienting it is. God says we reside at the very center of his eye—one of the most tender and sensitive parts of a person.

God puts himself within your reach through his promises to navigate life's difficulties with you. He isn't interested in being on the sidelines of your life; he wants to be in the trenches with you, helping you through your greatest challenges.

Living It Out 🌿 Close your eyes and imagine what it means to be the apple of God's eye. How does this perspective change how you see God's involvement in your waiting? Write down what came to mind.

• ——————— **Day 3 Prompt: Partnering with God** ——————— •

As a little girl, I loved movies like *Beauty and the Beast* and *Snow White and the Seven Dwarfs*. Now I gravitate toward romantic story lines such as *Sleepless in Seattle* and *You've Got Mail*. Pop culture molds much of our concepts about romantic relationships, with messaging that can bleed into our relationships, including with God.

The juxtaposition in our relationship with Jesus is that he is our Savior, but in order to experience him as such, we need to exercise our faith in him. We follow a similar pattern as we navigate seasons of waiting. God's active work in our lives doesn't negate the importance of our participation by taking risks and putting our faith into action.

Living It Out 🌿 In your relationship with God, how can you move away from a passive view toward a more active and engaged one? Perhaps by taking more risks on things you believe are from God? Or writing down your prayers and believing God will answer them even if he does so differently than you thought? Write down what comes to mind.

Day 4 Prompt: Getting Involved

How has the misguided idea about being a passive responder impacted your relationships with friends, coworkers, and family members? Have you believed your contributions weren't as important as theirs, so you didn't engage the way you wanted to?

What isn't said or done is equally as impactful as what is said or done. Passivity often leads to the deterioration of precious relationships. No matter how different our experiences, we need to be active participants in each other's lives, speaking into the hard places with hope and truth.

Living It Out 🌿 How can you be intentional this week to encourage someone in their waiting season? Could it be by being curious and asking good questions? Sending flowers or taking them for coffee? Notice who comes to mind and the ideas that form about how you can be more active in their lives.

The Promise of God's Presence

The Lord is like a father to his children,
tender and compassionate to those who fear him.
PSALM 103:13, NLT

AS A LITTLE GIRL, I loved tea parties with my dad. I would set the table with miniature cups and plates, and my big, grown-up dad would sit, pinkies up, and play tea party with me. Although there was no real tea or cookies, he was content to be my guest because he loved me and knew it brought me joy.

It wasn't until I was older that I understood how similarly our heavenly Father relates to us as his children.

I was twenty-five and heartbroken. The relationship I had built was over, and I was devastated. The abrupt ending sent my heart reeling.

One afternoon, I asked God, *If this relationship is going to turn around, please give me a sign.* After a while, I walked outside, and there, arcing across the sky in bold, beautiful colors, was my sign, the precise beauty I asked for. I felt God's tender presence as I savored the moment. Heaviness melted off my heart, and I could finally breathe again.

Time passed—a year and a half to be exact. I held tight to this moment with God until it was clear my hopes would not be realized. I was confused by circumstances that seemed to leave me holding an empty promise. As far as I knew, God didn't give promises he wasn't intent on keeping. I was at a sudden impasse with God and felt unsure where to go from there.

Clarity didn't come immediately. Eventually I moved to a new state, and God helped me understand this painful situation. In the process, I discovered a side to my heavenly Father I had only previously understood in my earthly one.

God reminded me of those tea parties with my dad. My dad wasn't being deceptive; he was meeting me where I was, in my capacity as a child. The kindest response was to join me, and one day I would understand there are real tea parties with real tea and cookies, and he would join me in those invitations too.

This display of God's kindness was equivalent to a father accepting an invitation to his daughter's tea party. God knew as time went on that I would discover what *I always knew* in my heart—that this relationship was never meant for me, similar to the realization that tea time with Dad never included real tea or cookies. I came to understand what God already knew—that I was clinging to this relationship out of pain, not desire.

I believe God fulfills every promise he makes, even when the unfolding looks unexpected. He did give me a promise that day. It was a promise of his presence in the moment, as well as a promise he would reveal over time—that he would be faithful to give me what I *really* wanted, and the promise to ultimately give what was best for me.

God does not comfort us with lies or deceit, but he does comfort us with his presence. The brilliant display in the sky that day was his way of taking a seat at his daughter's tea party and being present in her pain.

Genesis 32:24 tells of when God wrestled with Jacob all night long until the break of day. God could have ended this wrestling match in a millisecond. But Jacob needed this moment to arrive at surrender, as I did.

I remember those tea parties fondly, without feeling slighted. And when I remember that moment with God, I feel loved in ways I didn't know God could love me.

Perhaps you have felt confused by what appears to be an unfulfilled promise. I hope this simple story reminds you that God hears your cries and has unexpected ways of meeting your need.

Day 1 Prompt: Our True Desires

The article "The Importance of Pretend Play" explains experiences a child has during play, including nurturing imagination, developing language and cognitive skills, and growing in social and emotional capacities.[1]

Even in adulthood, we still need to deepen these fundamental skills, especially related to our faith. As God climbs into the proverbial sandbox with us, he displays profound sensitivity to us as his children. This act helps us grow. Our language expands, our faith deepens, and our capacity for empathy matures.

Living It Out 🌿 Reflect on an experience (or experiences) when God showed up in unusual ways and deepened your faith, expanded your language, and grew your emotional capacity.

———— Day 2 Prompt: Expanding Our Understanding ————

While on earth, Jesus looked for opportunities to expand people's ideas of what a life of faith looked like.

Our tendency as humans is to categorize everything. As we do, our perspectives become rigid, and we reduce the mystery of faith to a formula. Jesus seeks to disrupt our formulas and lead us into a deeper understanding of himself.

In the Sermon on the Mount (Matthew 5–7), Jesus breaks every religious box, addressing murder, adultery, divorce, vows, revenge, and much more. "You have heard the commandment that says, 'You must not commit adultery.' But I say, anyone who even looks at a woman with lust has already committed adultery with her in his heart" (Matthew 5:27-28, NLT). I'm sure that one ruffled some feathers.

In our waiting, God draws close to dispel our formulas and expand our understanding of himself.

Living It Out 🌿 Find a story in the Gospels when Jesus did something unexpected, and notice how he was expanding the understanding of those involved. Write down how this applies to your experience with God.

———— Day 3 Prompt: Letting the Dust Settle ————

Like me, you may have felt that your fervent prayers have bounced off the ceiling and hit you in the face. In 1 Kings 19, Elijah is desperately looking to God for answers, but God doesn't speak in the wind, earthquake, or fire. He speaks in a still, small voice.

Oftentimes we need to wait for the dust to settle and our hearts to hush before we can hear God clearly.

We will need to make many decisions to stay close to God when we don't understand. We can trust that as we settle our hearts, we will hear his still, small voice.

Living It Out 🌿 What stills your heart? Perhaps it's soaking in the quiet of the morning or taking an evening walk and breathing the cool air. Notice and write down what helps still you so you can hear God more clearly.

Day 4 Prompt: Healing in Community

It's not only time that brings healing. The people we spend *time with* become a means for deepest healing.

When a close friend shared her pain over a broken relationship, she expressed how the restoration she desired could only be achieved while immersed in a safe community. She could not heal in isolation.

I commended her for this wise perspective and affirmed that although some of her deepest hurts happened in relationships, her deepest healing could also happen in relationships.

Living It Out 🌿 There is a reason Jesus had a band of brothers. He knew some experiences are only possible together. "For wherever two or three come together in honor of my name, I am right there with them!" (Matthew 18:20). Reflect on this verse, and write down how your community can help usher in healing.

Relax, everything's
going to be all right;
rest, everything's coming
together; open your hearts,
love is on the way!

Jude 1:2, MSG

The Reality of Acceptance

Finding joy in the waiting does not mean you are giving up. It is saying, "This, right here is enough as I wait for what's to come."

MORGAN HARPER NICHOLS

WHEN I'M LISTENING TO A CLIENT'S STORY, I'm paying close attention to the words they use. Words are powerful, and we attach weighty associations *to* them based on our experiences *with* them.

When a word like *acceptance* continues to come up in a client's session, I'll grab my dry-erase board and do a simple word association with them. I write *acceptance* in the middle of the board and circle it. Then I ask the client to say whatever comes to mind when they think of acceptance. I draw a line from the word in the middle to each emotion, thought, and memory they say until we have what is known as a word web.

This visual allows them to see the ideas they associate with acceptance. One time a client responded with words like *complacency, approval, settling, apathy, defeat, giving up, fear, confusion.*

Acceptance can feel like a lofty idea that is impossible to implement. During seasons of waiting, acceptance can feel like defeat or giving up hope. I have felt frustrated when people talked about the importance of acceptance, because to me it felt like resignation.

If we're going to experience the peace associated with acceptance, we need to start by gathering evidence of its true meaning and eliminate what it *isn't* before we can understand what it *is*.

The English Oxford Dictionary defines *acceptance* as the "willingness to tolerate a difficult or unpleasant situation."[1] In twelve-step programs, the Serenity Prayer is at the heart of recovery and is a helpful mantra through temptations of relapse: "God grant me the Serenity to accept the things I cannot change, / Courage to change the things I can, and / Wisdom to know the difference."[2]

In Acceptance and Commitment Therapy (ACT), acceptance is understood as simply acknowledging reality, not necessarily approving of or resigning ourselves to that reality. And in his book *Coming to Our Senses: Healing Ourselves and the World through Mindfulness*, Jon Kabat-Zinn says this:

> Acceptance doesn't mean passive resignation. Quite the opposite. It takes a huge amount of fortitude and motivation to accept what is—especially when you don't like it—and then work wisely and effectively as best you possibly can . . . to mitigate, heal, redirect, and change what can be changed.[3]

If we navigate a waiting season with a skewed understanding of acceptance, we end up vacillating between striving for change and avoiding our circumstances.

Acceptance involves courage to acknowledge reality while maintaining hope. Hope isn't meant to shield us from acknowledging our current reality. It's designed to give us strength to believe there is something better beyond it.

As you wait, you can shed the false narratives about acceptance and experience the peace of acknowledging your present while maintaining hope for your future.

> Our present troubles are small and won't last very long. Yet they produce for us a glory that vastly outweighs them and will last forever!
> 2 CORINTHIANS 4:17, NLT

•——— Day 1 Prompt: Redefining Acceptance ———•

We can struggle with the false belief that waiting indicates we're either too much or not enough. Either belief keeps self-acceptance out of reach and creates false stories about our worthiness of being accepted.

Try the word-web exercise to unpack what you associate with acceptance. It will bring clarity to what you believe and the stories you've been telling yourself.

Living It Out 🌿 Open your journal and write *acceptance* in the middle of the page and circle it. Then write down anything you associate with acceptance, and draw a line to the center circle. It could be an emotion like fear or a thought like giving up. Take your time until there are lines with words all around the circle in the middle.

Take a few moments to notice the words that communicate the most powerful messages about acceptance. Choose one or two and write down the experiences in your life that may have led to associating these feelings, thoughts, or beliefs with acceptance.

Day 2 Prompt: Keeping the End in View

On a trip to Israel, I visited one of the locations where scholars believe Jesus was crucified. From that dusty site, our guide pointed in the distance and told us that across the mountain was Jesus' burial tomb. This meant that while Jesus was dying, he had a direct view of the place where he would rise from death. Hebrews 12:2 barreled into my mind: "For the joy [of accomplishing the goal] set before Him endured the cross, disregarding the shame" (AMP).

Jesus could literally see the goal of restored life and relationship as he endured the Cross. He kept the end in view and was strengthened to fulfill the plan of redemption.

Living It Out 🌿 What view would God want you to keep in mind to strengthen you with hope as you wait? As much as this view might be the tangible fulfillment of your prayers, could it also be the person you are becoming? Pray and journal what comes to mind.

Day 3 Prompt: Releasing Grief from Our Bodies

Waiting involves learning to navigate grief when painful things happen and when hoped-for things don't. It's not uncommon to hold grief in our bodies, which can show up as lethargy or tightness in the chest.

Grief expert Elisabeth Kübler-Ross says that one of the final stages of grief is acceptance.[4] The process isn't linear, and we move in and out of acceptance as we choose it again and again.

Every time we feel the pain of grief, we need to actively choose acceptance, and as my therapist says, we acknowledge the reality of grief without extinguishing hope.

Living It Out 🌿 Notice where your body might be holding grief. Is it in your chest, your stomach, your jaw? Close your eyes and breathe deeply until those places start to relax. Invite God into this experience, and notice how he replaces the burden of grief with hope and peace.

Day 4 Prompt: We're In This Together

A powerful aspect of twelve-step programs is the community they offer. Bill Wilson, cofounder of Alcoholics Anonymous, knew it was impossible to recover from addiction without a supportive community. Community is the ideal environment for ongoing recovery. Some of the most challenging times in my seasons of waiting have been when I was trying to manage pain on my own.

Acknowledging reality (aka acceptance) feels impossible when we're doing it alone. Acceptance is not only manageable but also sustainable when we're together.

We may not be recovering from addiction, but as we wait for significant change, we're faced with pain and the temptation to deny, avoid, and isolate. Just like the recovering addict who can't face these powerful forces alone, neither can we.

Living It Out 🌿 Write down the name of someone you trust when it comes to admitting your tendencies to withdraw, deny, or isolate. Reach out to them this week and share honestly about what you have been experiencing. Ask them to talk with you and figure out a plan together.

Where Would We Go?

Hear the sweet melody of your stillness, and the music that it gives.
JENNIFER WILLIAMSON, "BE STILL MY SOUL"

WHEN I WAS IN MY LATE TWENTIES, I got my first tattoo. It was inspired by a poem I read during one of my most difficult waiting seasons. The poem talks about musical rests and how unenjoyable a melody feels without them. It explains how every rest is full of purpose—it is the *making* of music, not the absence of it.

Many well-meaning people told me, "If you just let it go, it will happen." This commentary always triggered frustration in me and revealed two parallel beliefs, creating what psychologist Leon Festinger calls cognitive dissonance.

Cognitive dissonance is the mental and emotional discomfort we experience when we hold conflicting beliefs. Similar to an internal tug-of-war, we feel pushed and pulled in opposing directions.[1]

I believed God was involved in the details of my life, but I also felt disappointed by my circumstances. I started to believe that if I didn't make things happen, nothing would ever change. It was either me or God, not me and God.

My mind churned. *How can I let go of something that means so much to me? Doesn't letting go mean giving up? If I can't let go, am I getting in my own way? I have let go a thousand times, but nothing has changed!*

This dissonance reached a breaking point as I took a walk on a beautiful fall day. I felt crushed by disappointment and fear that my best efforts would never be enough and that God might never come through for me.

I poured out my heart as I walked along a quiet path in the woods. Despite the musical symbol etched on my wrist, my heart still couldn't rest. Rest felt like accepting defeat.

But then a fresh word pierced my turbulent thoughts. It was a passage of Scripture I hadn't thought of in years. Jesus' followers had been offended by his statements and were walking away. Jesus asks his twelve disciples if they, too, would go away.

"So Jesus said to his twelve, 'And you—do you also want to leave?' Peter spoke up and said, 'But Lord, where would we go? No one but you gives us the revelation of eternal life'" (John 6:67-68).

In beautiful honesty, Peter says, "Yes, we are offended too, but where would we go? Any life without you is no life at all."

Peter's question spoke directly to what I was feeling.

"Where would we go?" After years of waiting, these words helped my hurting heart find its way to true surrender. Through my tears I told God that even if he never gave me the family I desired, there would be no other place for me but with him.

Even if. These were big words for me, and ones I was never able to say until that moment. I had always negotiated with God: "I do this. You do that." It wasn't partnership, and it certainly wasn't surrender. It was conditional and transactional. For the first time I realized that although what I desired was valuable, staying connected to Jesus was even more important. As I walked along that quiet path in the woods, I found a place of rest, and it was in this resting that I finally "let go."

——— Day 1 Prompt: Rest Makes the Most Beautiful Melody ———

There is no music in a rest, but there is the making of music in it. In our whole life-melody the music is broken off here and there by "rests," and we foolishly think we have come to the end of the tune. God sends a time of forced leisure, sickness, disappointed plans, frustrated efforts, and makes a sudden pause in the choral hymn of our lives; and we lament that our voices must be silent, and our part missing in the music which ever goes up to the ear of the Creator. How does the musician read the "rest"? See him beat the time with

unvarying count, and catch up the next note true and steady, as if no breaking place had come between.[2]
JOHN RUSKIN

Living It Out 🌿 Reflect on the above portion of a poem by John Ruskin. Search for the January 22 entry for *Streams in the Desert* by L. B. Cowman to read it in its entirety. May it give you a new perspective on rest and impart the courage to entrust your desires to God.

Day 2 Prompt: Surrender to Rest

After I moved to California, one of my friends visited with her sweet baby. We went to the beach, and I offered to walk with the baby while she rested.

I assumed the sound of ocean waves would send him into dreamland, but they didn't. We walked up and down the shore until *I* was ready for a nap, but he refused to close his tired eyes and surrender to rest.

I saw myself in him. I desperately needed rest, but I wanted control, so I refused surrender. Perhaps you feel this way too. Perhaps you have been resisting your need to surrender and rest in God's arms.

Living It Out 🌿 Go for a walk and imagine you are tired, like this baby, but instead choose to surrender to the rest you need, allowing God to care for you while you wait.

Day 3 Prompt: God Wants to Collaborate

Cognitive dissonance can make it difficult for us to rest. We feel torn between two beliefs and assume answers come only with one or the other.

One belief claims, "God will take care of you, and he hasn't forgotten about you."

The other says, "Nothing has changed, so it's up to you now."

However, God values collaboration. The number of times the word *faith* is mentioned in Scripture confirms this. Faith is not all up to God or all up to you. Sometimes our part is to rest in God's arms while God fights for us. Other times, we're to take a faith-filled risk while God opens the doors.

Living It Out 🌿 Write down your conflicting beliefs around waiting, and then write the collaborative "both, and" version.

Day 4 Prompt: Learning to Trust God

In John 6:67-68, when many of Jesus' followers turn away from him, what strikes me is how Jesus presents each of his twelve disciples with a choice. Although they were part of a band of brothers, they still needed to make a personal decision to follow Jesus when it didn't make logical sense.

Amazingly, our personal decisions to rest in him, relinquish control, and trust him flow out and impact our relationships. When we choose to follow Jesus in our pain and confusion, we inspire people around us to trust God too. When we rest in God, surrendering to his heart of love toward us, we lend courage to those around us to do the same.

Living It Out 🌿 Consider those who have inspired you to trust God, and write down how you are doing that same thing for those around you.

The Last Will Be First

*The needy will not be ignored forever;
the hopes of the poor will not always be crushed.*

PSALM 9:18, NLT

THERE IS A STORY IN JOHN 5 of a crippled man who had lain by a pool called "The House of Loving Kindness" for thirty-eight years. This man had waited with hundreds of other sick people and experienced everything but kindness as he waited for healing.

Every so often, an angel would come down and stir the waters, and whoever stepped into the pool first would be healed. Honestly, this confused me initally, because it seemed to conflict with Jesus' words in Matthew 20:16: "The last will be first, and the first will be last" (NIV).

This man was so deteriorated by pain, he couldn't get to the water in time to be healed. Imagine him lying in this condition for thirty-eight years, watching person after person receive healing—all because they were quicker or more able.

Whatever your waiting story is, celebrating others' fulfilled desires and answered prayers—as yours go unfulfilled and unanswered—can be excruciating. I'm sure that for this man, sitting just out of reach of his healing and watching everyone else receive theirs drove him into despair.

Jesus sees the man and knows he has been crippled for a long time. His first question is, "Do you want to get well?" (John 5:6, NIV). As insensitive as this may seem, Jesus asked because he saw the hopelessness that had taken root in the man's heart.

"Sir, there's no way I can get healed, for I have no one to lower me into the

227

water when the angel comes. As soon as I try to crawl to the edge of the pool, someone else jumps in ahead of me" (verse 7).

Jesus doesn't argue or correct him. Instead, he offers *himself*. "Stand up! Pick up your sleeping mat and you will walk!" (verse 8). The man obeyed, was healed at last, and walked again.

Can you imagine the empowering dignity this moment offered? Jesus doesn't stir the water, pick him up, and put him in it to be healed. Jesus gives him much more than physical healing—he restores this man's dignity and emboldens him to stand up and pick up his mat himself. This man might have been the last to receive healing, but he was the first there to receive it the way he did—by partnering with Jesus to bring restoration to his broken heart and body.

Jesus cares about what we're waiting for, and he cares about restoring and depositing more than an answer. Maybe you are sitting by a proverbial pool, expecting it to be the only means for breakthrough. Perhaps the medium you're expecting God to use may not be the one he intends on using at all. When waiting is painful and you feel like you're "the last," God may be reserving an experience for you that will make you a *first*.

Day 1 Prompt: Two Different Approaches to Healing

Some of the best advice I received as a therapist came from my clinical supervisor. She likened my role to a guide carrying a flashlight in the dark. When my clients and I stumble into something significant in their stories, and the flashlight illuminates parts that have been hidden for a long time, I can either share what *I* see (directive approach) or ask what *they* see (guided approach).

The directive approach relies on the therapist as the expert and offers a perspective with potential to clear a path for new discovery. The guided approach relies on the client as the expert and challenges them to dig deeper to discover something new. In a similar fashion, Jesus guides the crippled man into healing and restores his dignity by empowering him to take hold of what has evaded him for so long.

Living It Out 🌿 In this summer season of waiting, what approach is God taking with you—directive or guided? What do you think he wants to give you in the process? Reflect and write down what comes to mind.

•——————— **Day 2 Prompt: Offering What You Have** ———————•

Matthew 14:13-18 describes a time when Jesus tries to slip away to recharge, but the crowd follows him. Because of his compassion, he spends all day healing everyone who is sick.

As it gets late, the disciples tell Jesus to send the people away to eat. Jesus replies, "You give them something to eat" (verse 16, NIV).

When they answer, "We have here only five loaves of bread and two fish" (verse 17, NIV), Jesus instructs them to bring the bread and fish to him, and with it he feeds the multitude.

Jesus wasn't interested in showing off his powers. He was interested in showing his disciples how much power *they* had in the situation. Jesus was teaching them to offer what they had, and together they could do something miraculous.

Living It Out 🌿 How is God inviting you to partner with him? Journal, walk, or pray as you reflect on these questions.

•——————— **Day 3 Prompt: The Way Out** ———————•

Waiting can be both humbling and humiliating, and sometimes it's difficult to discern the difference. Often, feeling humbled is tied to an experience of humility, whereas feeling humiliated is tied to an experience of shame. Waiting encourages dependence on God, which is humbling, but waiting can feel humiliating when it drags on and defers our hope.

Shame, pride, and humility are connected, and as we navigate the challenges of waiting, we will cycle through all three. Shame assumes our waiting results from some flaw or failure. Pride leads to hardening our hearts to protect ourselves. But we experience humility when we allow ourselves to be imperfect and partner with God through the difficult moments.

The man in John 5 probably felt crippling shame. But when he availed himself to receive healing, he bravely chose humility over shame and pride.

Living It Out 🌿 Does shame, pride, or humility feel more prominent to you now? Write down how humility can be a way out of shame or pride.

———— **Day 4 Prompt: Remembering Each Other** ————

One of my close friends, Hannah, got married in 2020, when the size of gatherings was limited. Only a handful of people attended the intimate ceremony, and it made me keenly aware of the tension in my heart between joy for my friend and sorrow for myself.

During the reception, she and I had a few moments to connect. She grabbed my hand and said, "I know this is hard, and I see you." She said other beautiful things as tears streamed down my face.

She didn't have to acknowledge my pain in the middle of her joy, but she remembered what it was like to be in my position. She went out of her way to see me and the grief I carried.

Living It Out 🌿 Sometimes you are the one experiencing joy, and other times, the one grieving. Let's commit to seeing others who are in different seasons than our own. Pray, reflect, and journal what comes to mind.

Waiting for a Change

*While you are waiting, you are not merely waiting. You are growing in
your capacity to receive what was meant for you in the right timing.*

MORGAN HARPER NICHOLS

I WAS A PART OF THE SAME COMMUNITY from the time I was a baby until I was
twenty-nine years old. Then in 2012, a significant shift began in my heart.
Although I didn't understand it, I remember moments of a strong and sudden
sense that God wanted me to be prepared for something new.

God was slowly uprooting my heart from the life I had always known and
the one I had envisioned—being a part of the church I had grown up in and
one day settling down with someone in that community. As time went on, it
became apparent that might not be God's intention.

I was picking up the pieces after a devastating breakup, feeling like I had
hit a wall, lost and desperate for a fresh start. At the end of 2012, I enrolled
in an online biblical counseling program, and during the next couple of years,
this sense from God became stronger and more specific.

In spring of 2014, I had a strong feeling that I would not be in Baltimore
that fall. I didn't share this with anyone because there were no prospects on
the horizon to make sense of something so specific.

In addition to my counseling program, I was learning about the devastating issue of human trafficking and discovered an organization based in
California called The A21 Campaign.

I needed to do a counseling internship, and one evening while waiting at
the airport to board my flight, something at the gate reminded me of A21.

I found their website and landed on a page about open internship opportunities. So I applied, closed my laptop, and boarded my flight.

Three days later, I received an email asking me to set up an interview, and a week after that, I received another email saying I had been accepted for the internship—in California. I sat in my car, bubbling over with tears of gratitude and joy. The last two years of waiting for God to make a way had been trying and painful. The gift of an opportunity to dream up a completely different life filled me in a way I had never experienced.

You know the most amazing part? My internship began September 1. Just as God had said, I was no longer in Baltimore that fall.

The summer seasons of waiting are full of anticipation for what's next, which often makes exercising patience seem nearly impossible. Waiting for the page to turn in life can feel exhausting. Knowing there is much more for us challenges us to keep going and not give up. C. S. Lewis said, "There are far better things ahead than any we leave behind."[1] While waiting for these "far better things," we can learn faithfulness where we are, while keeping our ears attentive to God's voice until the path clears to move forward confidently.

Keep your eyes, ears, and heart open. God sees you. He hasn't overlooked your longing. Be expectant, and bravely choose to keep your hopes up.

⸻ Day 1 Prompt: The Past, Present, and Future ⸻

As a trauma therapist, I've learned how interconnected the past, present, and future are. For instance, someone who is diagnosed with post-traumatic stress disorder will often experience reactions that have everything to do with the past. If someone with PTSD hears a loud crash, their heart might race, or they could sweat or feel the need to run away. The sound is not the real issue; it triggers the brain's fight-or-flight response, which registers a threat.

It's easy to project a painful experience onto the future and assume that what is to come will look just like our past. It's important to be mindful not to let our past determine what we believe is possible in our futures.

Living It Out 🌿 Have painful experiences made it difficult to hope? Take inventory of the events in your past and present that you may be projecting onto your future. Allow yourself to see these experiences as separate from your future, and allow God to give you hope and expectation for what's to come.

Day 2 Prompt: Experience Is Key

When I was a younger Christian, I was confused by language like "walking by faith" and "being led by the Spirit." These essential principles in Christianity can be challenging to embody and live out.

Experience is powerful, and once we experience living "in step" with the Holy Spirit, it's no longer just a nice idea. Taking brave action puts knowledge into motion and brings important change. We will be challenged this way time and again. By living close to God, we learn to recognize a sacred sense to move forward, even when we're scared.

Psalm 34:8 says, "Taste and see that the LORD is good" (NIV). Tasting and seeing the Lord's goodness have potential to dramatically expand our perceptions of waiting seasons so we can anticipate the possibilities all around us.

Living It Out 🌿 Reflect on a concept in your faith that has been difficult to put into practice. Consider an experience while waiting that has positively impacted you and given you strength for the present and hope for the future.

Day 3 Prompt: Growing in Faithfulness

The whole idea of being faithful where you are, while you're waiting, is character-building. Luke 16:10 says, "If you are faithful in little things, you will be faithful in large ones" (NLT).

As we are faithful in our current seasons, we are growing our capacities. Showing up to face the unglamorous moments in our jobs, families, and communities develops our character and causes us to grow in the faithfulness that makes us trustworthy people.

Living It Out 🌿 What are you being trusted with right now? How can your faithfulness make you trustworthy to hold all that God wants to give you? Write down what comes to mind.

Day 4 Prompt: Holding Space for Hope and Pain

One of the greatest gifts we can offer each other is the hope to believe that life can look better than it might now. We are so close to our own lives that we easily lose sight of who we really are and what is possible. We can validate each other's pain while offering reminders that, no matter how hard life is now, we *can* experience hope and joy again.

I remember a time when one of my clients was struggling to believe life was still worth living. Hopeless negativity filled their thoughts and self-talk. After a few moments of silent space to honor the pain, I explained how the trauma was eclipsing their view of themselves. As they experienced healing, they would be able to see themselves as they really are—worthy and enough.

Living It Out 🌿 How can you extend hope to others while holding space for their pain? If someone has done this for you, how did it give you hope and strength to keep going? Reflect on these questions, and write down what comes to mind.

You're Closer than You Think

Relax, everything's going to be all right; rest, everything's coming together;
open your hearts, love is on the way!

JUDE 1:2, MSG

FOR SOME REASON, I love going through the car wash. It transports me back to when I was a little girl sitting in the back seat of my parents' car, watching the funny contraptions move all over the vehicle.

One afternoon, as I arrived in my very dirty car at the nearest car wash, I thought about how peculiar the process is. Every part has a different purpose. One hose wets your vehicle, another sprays colorful bubbles, and spaghetti-like sponges move the soap and water around.

Near the end, the force of air was so intense that my car started shaking. I reminded myself that this was just the last stage of the process. It sparked the thought that in any refining process (like waiting), the last stage always feels the most intense.

Think about runners nearing the end of a marathon. Their lungs are burning, their muscles are depleted, and their mouths are parched from dehydration. Research shows that once your body reaches glycogen depletion—meaning you have burned through your energy stores—it scrambles to metabolize fat. Your legs and arms feel like logs, and your brain tells you to quit.

Similarly, the process of waiting feels most intense when you're nearing the end, and the temptation to quit is strong. All you know is that it's hard, and you cannot imagine taking another step.

As I sat there in my car, I sensed God saying that every part of my process had been necessary, and this last part felt the most intense because it was drying off the residue.

As we move through seasons of waiting, many weights that don't belong attach themselves to us: lies about our worth, the pain of disappointment, feeling abandoned by God, and much more. God sees this residue and cares about removing it before we're fully released. If you've reached the end of your resources, you're closer than you think to driving out of that proverbial car wash and into the sunlight.

I'm not ending this devotional by saying, "And then they all lived happily ever after." But I am saying that this pain will *not* last forever, and most importantly, that the process is full of purpose.

It has deepened, healed, and transformed you. It has taught you to cling to what is good and release what is not. It has removed what has eclipsed your view of who you are to reveal your depth, beauty, and worthiness. When you exit this last stage, you will not only be a more whole version of yourself but also free of residue that has built up around your heart.

"Weeping may last through the night, but joy comes with the morning" (Psalm 30:5, NLT). Joy is coming. Love is on its way. And hope is already here.

— Day 1 Prompt: Hope Is a Companion —

My friend Joanna told me about a church conference she attended where one of the speakers addressed the topic of hope. She said that when we use the phrase "Hope is on the way," we typically imagine hope as something that "arrives" in our lives. She then offered a new perspective of hope as a companion. If we understand hope only as something coming *to* us, we forfeit the comfort of hope journeying *with* us.

The two men on the road to Emmaus had no idea that Jesus was walking with them as they poured out their grief about his death and their loss of hope. When Jesus finally revealed himself to them, they were able to look back and see that hope had been walking with them the whole time (Luke 24:13-35).

Living It Out ꙮ How does this perspective impact how you think about hope? Write down what comes to mind.

Day 2 Prompt: Removing the Residue

I grew up hearing the story about the three Hebrew boys Shadrach, Meshach, and Abednego. They were thrown into a fiery furnace for their faith, and they not only survived but also walked out completely unscathed.

> Nebuchadnezzar went to the door of the roaring furnace and called in, "Shadrach, Meshach, and Abednego, servants of the High God, come out here!" Shadrach, Meshach, and Abednego walked out of the fire. . . . The fire hadn't so much as touched the three men—not a hair singed, not a scorch mark on their clothes, not even the smell of fire on them!
>
> DANIEL 3:26-27, MSG

God cares about removing even the faintest "smell of fire"—the residue of resentment, disappointment, and shame—from our hearts. This doesn't mean we don't remember the pain we endured or that we walk out of difficulties squeaky clean. It means God is interested in removing anything that might hold us back from experiencing abundant life.

Living It Out 🌿 What residue do you think God wants to remove from your heart and mind? Reflect and pray, asking God how he wants to remove this residue.

Day 3 Prompt: Revealing the Brilliance Underneath

Have you ever heard of lapidaries? They are artists skilled in the best techniques for cutting stones, removing the excess, and revealing a jewel's brilliance. June Culp Zeitner says, "What a true lapidary artist needs is an eye for beauty, originality, and excellent craftsmanship."[1]

Expert lapidaries don't create beauty; they reveal existing beauty. And like the lapidary who cuts away the excess with sharp instruments, God removes the residue in your life to reveal the beauty hidden underneath. The removal can hurt and at times appears cruel and thoughtless. But we choose to trust the veracity of God's heart and believe that he is revealing beauty in us.

Living It Out ❧ Imagine yourself as a jewel and God as the lapidary. Imagine him observing you with love and intention as he skillfully cuts away what doesn't belong to reveal the brilliance underneath. How does this picture relate to your seasons of waiting? Reflect on this and journal what you notice.

Day 4 Prompt: Cheering Each Other On

When I think about running a marathon, my first thought is that I might die, and my second thought is about how important those people are who cheer from the sidelines.

A runner in their last couple of miles is in desperate need of encouragement. The crowd of people toward the end can give them the boost of confidence to finish. We need each other to complete our seasons of waiting.

When we're running on fumes and exhausted, we need to speak hope and faith into each other. We need to tell each other to keep going when every fiber of our being wants to give up. We need to remind each other that we are worth the struggle and we aren't alone. And we need to hold up a mirror to remind each other how beautiful we are when all we see and feel is the blood, sweat, and tears.

Living It Out ❧ Think of someone who may be running on fumes, and pray about how you could encourage that person this week.

As I'm sure you know, waiting is a unique *and* universal human experience. I also hope you know by now that you aren't alone in the journey. Your story matters, and it is unfolding in stunning ways with every moment that passes. Be brave as you step into the wait as a worthy and empowered participant with God. As you engage each season of waiting, do so with hope and the conviction that you will "see the goodness of the LORD in the land of the living" (Psalm 27:13, NIV).

The LORD is like a father
to his children, tender
and compassionate to
those who fear him.

Psalm 103:13, NLT

Acknowledgments

Writing a book takes a village, and I'm deeply grateful for mine. I didn't arrive at this opportunity without the love and belief of so many, and I'm grateful to honor a few of them here.

To my friend and gifted artist, Shealeen: Thank you from the bottom of my heart for believing in this project from day one. You walked the peaks and valleys of this process with me and never wavered in your belief in me or in this book. I love you.

To the amazing team at Tyndale: Thank you for believing in me and in the message of this book. Through every difficulty we were thrown, you continued to lean in and help us face the challenges together. Thank you for your commitment to see this book come to fruition.

To my friend and incredible writing consultant, Beth: I would have been lost without you. From voice texts to emails and phone calls, you generously gave of yourself as a friend and professional, and I am so grateful.

To my wildly talented editor, Erin: Thank you for going above and beyond in the editing of this book. You met each challenge with honesty and integrity, and working with you has made me a better writer.

To my parents: Words fall short, but I'll try. Thank you for your steadfast belief in me. You have lived this book with me. You have prayed with me, wiped my tears, and reminded me to keep believing. I love you.

To my small group—Savannah, Sarah, Tara, Catherine, and Jamie: Thank you for proofreading and choosing your favorite devotions in the early days, in hopes that this book would find its way into the world. Thank you for always holding the safest space for me to unfurl my heart. Thank you for believing in me and carrying me through some of my darkest times and for celebrating with me on the brightest days. I love you.

Thank you to Hannah Kaul for being my biggest cheerleader and for holding up my hands when they were tired.

Thank you to Hannah Muñoz for standing by my side as a friend and as a brilliant writer. You stepped in when I needed you most, and I am so grateful.

Thank you to Becky for always believing in me from my early blog days and encouraging me to take the steps that ultimately led to this book.

Thank you to Elizabeth for our Post-it days and for helping me make sense of all my ideas.

Thank you to Grace and Lisa for being friends in every season. You have seen me through so many. I love you.

Thank you to Joanna for that conversation many years ago that sparked the devotional that led me here. You are a gift to me.

Thank you to Becca for your empathy and listening ear. You walked out much of this book with me, and I'll never forget our days on Gracious Drive. Love you.

Thank you to Deb for believing in me as a therapist from day one and making a way for that dream to be realized. You have played a significant role in shaping me as a therapist and as a writer.

Thank you to Bianca for those early days in the A21 California office. Thank you for seeing my raw potential and opening doors to exercise and hone my gifts. Your love and belief have paved the way for countless opportunities. I'm forever grateful. I love you.

Thank you, Jesus, for your faithful friendship. Thank you for your commitment to my healing and growth as well as to the fulfillment of my heart's desires. Thank you for loving me the same on my worst days as you do on my best. Thank you for showing me what a true relationship with you looks like and for empowering me to live out each day with freedom, peace, and joy in the waiting.

Lastly, I'm so grateful to each of you who have picked up this book. Thank you for your willingness to be challenged, encouraged, and transformed. I hope this book becomes one of your most beloved companions as you journey through this life.

Love,
Barb

Notes

AUTHOR'S NOTE

1. Naval Ravikant, quoted in James Clear, *Atomic Habits: An Easy & Proven Way to Build Good Habits & Break Bad Ones* (New York: Avery, 2018), 8.
2. "Four Sons," in Norma Boone, *Morning Dew Drops: Bloom Where You Are Planted* (Bloomington, IN: WestBow, 2020).
3. Ernest Hemingway, *A Moveable Feast* (New York: Charles Scribner's Sons, 1964), 45.

WEEK ONE

1. Brené Brown, *Daring Greatly: How the Courage to Be Vulnerable Transforms the Way We Live, Love, Parent, and Lead* (London: Penguin Books Limited, 2013), n.p.
2. Curt Thompson, *The Soul of Shame: Retelling the Stories We Believe about Ourselves* (Downers Grove, IL: IVP, 2015), 124–25, emphasis mine.
3. Oswald Chambers, *My Utmost for His Highest, updated language* (Grand Rapids, MI: Our Daily Bread, 2010), September 12.
4. "Collective Effervescence," Wikipedia, accessed October 24, 2021, https://en.wikipedia.org/wiki/Collective_effervescence.
5. Émile Durkheim, *The Elementary Forms of the Religious Life, trans. Joseph Ward Swain* (London: George Allen & Unwin, 1915), 249, https://auro-ebooks-in.s3.ap-south-1.amazonaws.com/book-uploads/Emile-Durkheim-The-Elementary-Forms-of-the-Religious-Life.pdf.

WEEK TWO

1. *Merriam-Webster.com Dictionary*, s.v. "wait," accessed November 30, 2021, https://www.merriam-webster.com/dictionary/wait.
2. Albert Bandura, "Agency," Albert Bandura, accessed October 25, 2021, https://albertbandura.com/albert-bandura-agency.html.
3. Bandura, "Agency."
4. Chong Singsit, "The Scientific Basis of Seed Germination as Revealed in Scripture," Kuki International Forum, December 27, 2008, http://kukiforum.com/2008/12/the-scientific-basis-of-seed-germination-as-revealed-in-scripture-2/.

WEEK THREE

1. Brené Brown, "Brené Brown on How to Reckon with Emotion and Change Your Narrative," Oprah.com, September 17, 2015 issue of *O, The Oprah Magazine*, https://www.oprah.com/omagazine/brene-brown-rising-strong-excerpt.
2. Leo Widrich, "The Science of Storytelling: What Listening to a Story Does to Our Brains," Buffer (blog), November 29, 2012, https://buffer.com/resources/science-of-storytelling-why-telling-a-story-is-the-most-powerful-way-to-activate-our-brains/.

WEEK FOUR

1. "Projection," *Psychology Today*, accessed October 26, 2021, https://www.psychologytoday.com/us/basics/projection.
2. Bill Gaultiere, "'Fear Not!' 365 Days a Year," Soul Shepherding, accessed November 22, 2021, https://www.soulshepherding.org/fear-not-365-days-a-year/.
3. Richard Rohr, "A Hidden Wholeness," Center for Action and Contemplation, January 26, 2020, https://cac.org/a-hidden-wholeness-2020-01-26/.
4. Alicia Britt Chole, *Anonymous: Jesus' Hidden Years . . . and Yours* (Nashville: Thomas Nelson, 2011), 27.

WEEK FIVE

1. Michelle L. Buck, "The Power of 'Both-And' Thinking," *Psychology Today*, October 22, 2020, https://www.psychologytoday.com/us/blog/unleashing-the-potential/202010/the-power-both-and-thinking.
2. Martin B. Copenhaver, *Jesus Is the Question: The 307 Questions Jesus Asked and the 3 He Answered* (Nashville: Abingdon Press, 2014).

WEEK SIX

1. "A Beginner's Guide to Understanding Bible Translations," South Bay Bible Church, accessed October 26, 2021, https://www.southbaychurchli.org/life-purpose-hope-blog/a-beginners-guide-to-understanding-bible-translations.

WEEK SEVEN

1. Vienna Pharaon (@mindfulmft), Instagram meme, July 18, 2021.
2. Henri J. M. Nouwen, *Bread for the Journey: A Daybook of Wisdom and Faith* (New York: HarperOne, 2006), 4.
3. Brett and Kate McKay, "The Power of Conversation: A Lesson from CS Lewis and JRR Tolkien," The Art of Manliness, June 3, 2021, https://www.artofmanliness.com/character/manly-lessons/the-power-of-conversation-a-lesson-from-cs-lewis-and-jrr-tolkien/.

WEEK EIGHT

1. Mark Nepo, *The Book of Awakening: Having the Life You Want by Being Present to the Life You Have* (Newburyport, MA: Red Wheel, 2020), 230.
2. Saul McLeod, "Attachment Theory," Simply Psychology, February 5, 2017, https://www.simplypsychology.org/attachment.html.

WEEK NINE

1. "Captain" by Seth Simmons and Benjamin Hastings. Copyright © 2015 Hillsong Music Publishing (APRA) (adm. in the US and Canada at CapitolCMGPublishing.com). All rights reserved. Used by permission.
2. Kendra Cherry, "Locus of Control and Your Life," Verywell Mind, August 16, 2021, https://www.verywellmind.com/what-is-locus-of-control-2795434.

WEEK TEN

1. L. B. Cowman, "Streams in the Desert—October 3," Crosswalk.com, October 3, 2021, https://www.crosswalk.com/devotionals/desert/streams-in-the-desert-october-3rd.html.

WEEK ELEVEN

1. Written by Jesse Reeves, Chris Tomlin, and Martin Smith. Copyright © 2011 Thankyou Music (PRS) (adm. worldwide at CapitolCMGPublishing.com, excluding the UK & Europe, which is adm. at IntegratedRights.com) / worshiptogether.com; Songs (ASCAP); sixsteps Music (ASCAP); Vamos Publishing (ASCAP); Gloworks Limited (PRS) (adm. at CapitolCMGPublishing.com). All rights reserved. Used by permission.
2. Gretchen Rubin, "The Psychology of Waiting: 8 Factors that Make the Wait Seem Longer," Psych Central, October 19, 2012, https://psychcentral.com/blog/the-psychology-of-waiting-in-lines-8-reasons-that-the-wait-seems-long#1.
3. Caroline Leaf, "The Effect of Worship on the Brain and General Health," Joy! Digital, accessed November 24, 2021, https://www.joydigitalmag.com/voice-post/the-effect-of-worship-on-the-brain-and-general-health/.

WEEK TWELVE

1. Kendra Cherry, "What Is Object Permanence?" Verywell Mind, April 19, 2021, https://www.verywellmind .com/what-is-object-permanence-2795405.
2. L. B. Cowman, "Streams in the Desert – October 9," Crosswalk.com, October 9, 2021, https://www.crosswalk .com/devotionals/desert/streams-in-the-desert-october-9th.html.

WEEK THIRTEEN

1. Bessel A. van der Kolk, *The Body Keeps the Score: Brain, Mind, and Body in the Healing of Trauma* (New York: Penguin Books, 2014), 79.
2. "How Box Breathing Can Help You Destress," Cleveland Clinic, August 17, 2021, https://health.clevelandclinic .org/box-breathing-benefits/.
3. Katherine May, *Wintering: The Power of Rest and Retreat in Difficult Times* (New York: Riverhead Books, 2020), 43.

WEEK FOURTEEN

1. Teresa of Avila, "Christ Has No Body," Journey with Jesus, accessed October 29, 2021, https:// www.journeywithjesus.net/PoemsAndPrayers/Teresa_Of_Avila_Christ_Has_No_Body.shtml.

WEEK FIFTEEN

1. Merriam-Webster.com Dictionary, s.v. "anticipation," accessed December 2, 2021, https://www.merriam-webster .com/dictionary/anticipation .
2. Neil Patel, "The Psychology of Anticipation and What It Means for Your Conversion Rates," Unbounce, July 14, 2014, https://unbounce.com/conversion-rate-optimization/psychology-of-anticipation-conversion-rates/.
3. Victor Knowles, "Promise and Fulfillment: Believing the Promises of God," Leaven 6, no. 3: (January 1, 1998): article 4, https://digitalcommons.pepperdine.edu/leaven/vol6/iss3/4.
4. *Merriam-Webster.com Dictionary*, s.v. "promise," accessed December 2, 2021, https://www.merriam-webster .com/dictionary/promise.
5. Kendra Cherry, "What Is Group Therapy?" Verywell Mind, July 13, 2021, https://www.verywellmind.com/what -is-group-therapy-2795760.

WEEK SIXTEEN

1. Marc Brackett, *Permission to Feel: Unlocking the Power of Emotions to Help Our Kids, Ourselves, and Our Society Thrive* (New York: Celadon Books, 2019), 22.
2. Matthew Richard Schlimm, "Emotions and Faith: The Perplexing Relationship between What We Feel and What We Believe," Columbia Theological Seminary, accessed October 27, 2021, https://www.ctsnet.edu/at-this-point /emotions-faith-perplexing-relationship-feel-believe/.

WEEK SEVENTEEN

1. Brené Brown, "Brené Brown on Empathy," RSA, December 10, 2013, YouTube video, 2:53, https://www.youtube .com/watch?v=1Evwgu369Jw.
2. A. J. Adams, "Seeing Is Believing: The Power of Visualization," *Psychology Today*, December 3, 2009, https:// www.psychologytoday.com/us/blog/flourish/200912/seeing-is-believing-the-power-visualization.

WEEK EIGHTEEN

1. Stephanie Kirby, "Fight Flight Freeze: How to Recognize It and What to Do When It Happens," BetterHelp, January 13, 2021, https://www.betterhelp.com/advice/trauma/fight-flight-freeze-how-to-recognize-it-and-what -to-do-when-it-happens/.

WEEK NINETEEN

1. "History of EMDR," EMDR Institute, accessed November 29, 2021, https://www.emdr.com/history-of-emdr/.
2. Brené Brown, "Own Our History. Change the Story," Brené Brown, June 18, 2015, https://brenebrown.com/blog /2015/06/18/own-our-history-change-the-story/.
3. Daniel P. Brown, "About Dr. Daniel P. Brown," Dr. Daniel P. Brown, accessed October 27, 2021, https:// www.drdanielpbrown.com/daniel-brown.

WEEK TWENTY
1. "Fullness (Patch) (4138) Pleroma," SermonIndex.net, accessed October 25, 2021, https://www.sermonindex.net/modules/articles/index.php?view=article&aid=34125.

WEEK TWENTY-ONE
1. This idea about grief is paraphrased from an unknown *Typology* podcast by Ian Cron that I listened to two years before this writing.
2. Lynn Rossy, "Riding the Waves of Grief," Lynn Rossy, accessed November 29, 2021, https://www.lynnrossy.com/riding-the-waves-of-grief/.
3. David Guzik, "Psalm 88—A Desperate Prayer from Deep Affliction," Enduring Word, accessed November 29, 2021, https://enduringword.com/bible-commentary/psalm-88/.
4. Charles H. Spurgeon, "The Treasury of David, Psalm 88," The Spurgeon Archives, accessed December 3, 2021, https://archive.spurgeon.org/treasury/ps088.php.
5. Erin Coriell, "Grieving in Community," HuffPost, March 4, 2017, https://www.huffpost.com/entry/grieving-in-community_b_9371060.

WEEK TWENTY-TWO
1. Christopher J. Colvin, *Traumatic Storytelling and Memory in Post-Apartheid South Africa: Performing Signs of Injury* (London: Routledge, 2018).
2. Alice Miller, "The Essential Role of an Enlightened Witness in Society," Alice Miller, 1997, https://www.alice-miller.com/en/the-essential-role-of-an-enlightened-witness-in-society/.
3. Frances Bridges, "The Best of Maya Angelou," *Forbes*, May 28, 2014, https://www.forbes.com/sites/francesbridges/2014/05/28/the-best-of-maya-angelou/?sh=788f70802f4e.
4. Christopher Hudson, *100 Names of God Daily Devotional* (Peabody, MA: Rose, 2019).

WEEK TWENTY-THREE
1. Paul Tillich, *The Eternal Now* (New York: Charles Scribner's Sons, 1963), 5, https://antilogicalism.com/wp-content/uploads/2017/07/the-eternal-now.pdf.
2. Hannah Hippe, "Being Lonely and Being Alone: What's the Difference?" Nystrom & Associates, February 4, 2021, https://www.nystromcounseling.com/mental-health/being-lonely-and-being-alone-whats-the-difference/.

WEEK TWENTY-SIX
1. Richard Rohr, "Oneing: Introduction," *Oneing* 8, no. 1, posted at Center for Action and Contemplation, April 26, 2020, https://cac.org/oneing-liminal-space-introduction/.
2. Richard Rohr, "Liminal Space," Transformation: Week Two, Center for Action and Contemplation, July 7, 2016, https://cac.org/liminal-space-2016-07-07/.
3. Debbie Daltrey, "What Are Neural Pathways?" *Great Minds Clinic* (blog), accessed March 20, 2021, https://www.greatmindsclinic.co.uk/blog/what-are-neural-pathways/.
4. Ashley Mead, "How Big Life Transitions Impact Your Mental Health," myTherapyNYC, September 12, 2019, https://mytherapynyc.com/managing-life-transitions-impact-mental-health/.

WEEK TWENTY-EIGHT
1. Bart de Langhe, Stefano Puntoni, and Richard Larrick, "Linear Thinking in a Nonlinear World," *Harvard Business Review*, accessed November 30, 2021, https://hbr.org/2017/05/linear-thinking-in-a-nonlinear-world.
2. See Philip Yancey, *What's So Amazing about Grace?* (Grand Rapids, MI: Zondervan, 1997), 45.
3. Kira M. Newman, "How Comforting Others Helps You with Your Own Struggles," *Greater Good Magazine*, June 5, 2017, https://greatergood.berkeley.edu/article/item/how_comforting_others_helps_you_with_your_own_struggles.

WEEK TWENTY-NINE
1. Amanda Lindsey Cook, Jason Ingram, and Paul Mabury, "Heroes," Bethel Music, accessed December 2, 2020, https://bethelmusic.com/chords-and-lyrics/brave-new-world-heroes/. "Heroes" is written by Amanda Cook, Jason Ingram, and Paul Mabury. Copyright © 2015 Bethel Music Publishing (ASCAP)/So Essential Tunes/Open Hands Music (SESAC) (adm. by Essential Music Publishing LLC)/So Essential Tunes (SESAC)/Flychild Publishing (SESAC) (adm. by Essential Music Publishing LLC). All rights reserved.

2. Richard Rohr, "At Home in Mystery," Center for Action and Contemplation, August 24, 2016, https://cac.org/at-home-in-mystery-2016-08-24/.
3. Brené Brown, *Daring Greatly: How the Courage to Be Vulnerable Transforms the Way We Live, Love, Parent, and Lead* (London: Penguin Books Limited, 2013), 113.

WEEK THIRTY

1. *Merriam-Webster.com Dictionary*, s.v. "complicated," accessed December 7, 2021, https://www.merriam-webster.com/dictionary/complicated.
2. *Merriam-Webster.com Dictionary*, s.v. "complex," accessed December 7, 2021, https://www.merriam-webster.com/dictionary/complex.
3. Theodore Kinni, "The Critical Difference between Complex and Complicated," MIT Sloan Management Review, June 21, 2017, https://sloanreview.mit.edu/article/the-critical-difference-between-complex-and-complicated/.
4. Kinni, "The Critical Difference between Complex and Complicated."
5. Cooper P. Abrams III, "Mysteries of the Bible," September 2000, https://bible-truth.org/myst-intro.htm.
6. Kendra Cherry, "What Is a Mindset and Why It Matters," Verywell Mind, April 29, 2021, https://www.verywellmind.com/what-is-a-mindset-2795025.
7. DJ Edwardson, "The Tapestry Poem," djedwardson.com, January 6, 2015, https://djedwardson.com/tapestry-poem/.

WEEK THIRTY-ONE

1. M. Dittmann, "Chronic Second-Guessing Jeopardizes Mental Health," American Psychological Association, May 2003, https://www.apa.org/monitor/may03/chronic.html.

WEEK THIRTY-TWO

1. Dan Taylor, "The Life-Shaping Power of Story: God's and Ours," Desiring God, September 27, 2008, https://www.desiringgod.org/messages/the-life-shaping-power-of-story-gods-and-ours.

WEEK THIRTY-THREE

1. Frank Han, "How the Brain Saves Energy: The Neural Thermostat," Yale Scientific, September 1, 2010, https://www.yalescientific.org/2010/09/how-the-brain-saves-energy-the-neural-thermostat/.
2. Matthew D. Lieberman, et al., "Putting Feelings into Words: Affect Labeling Disrupts Amygdala Activity in Response to Affective Stimuli," Psychological Science 18, no. 5 (May 2007): 421–28, https://pubmed.ncbi.nlm.nih.gov/17576282/.
3. James W. Pennebaker, "Writing about Emotional Experiences as a Therapeutic Process," Psychological Science 8, no. 3 (May 1997): 162–66, http://www.jstor.org/stable/40063169.

WEEK THIRTY-FIVE

1. Rachel Anyika, "How Emotional Attunement Can Transform Your Relationships," Emotion Enhancement, October 14, 2018, https://www.emotionenhancement.com/single-post/how-attunement-can-transform-your-relationships.
2. Merv Knight, "Tortured for Christ," Christian History Institute, accessed November 23, 2021, https://christianhistoryinstitute.org/magazine/article/tortured-for-christ.

WEEK THIRTY-SIX

1. Bridget Freer, "What Is the 'Anniversary Effect'? And What to Do If You Have It," The Awareness Centre, accessed December 6, 2021, https://theawarenesscentre.com/what-is-the-anniversary-effect/.
2. Lisa Fritscher, "Coping with Anticipatory Anxiety," Verywell Mind, March 9, 2020, https://www.verywellmind.com/anticipatory-anxiety-2671554.
3. "Jack Needs Jill to Get Up the Hill: Perceptions Affected by Friendship," *Virginia Magazine*, accessed December 24, 2021, https://uvamagazine.org/articles/jack_needs_jill_to_get_up_the_hill.

WEEK THIRTY-SEVEN

1. Mark Nepo, *The Book of Awakening: Having the Life You Want by Being Present to the Life You Have* (Newburyport, MA: Red Wheel, 2020), 102.

2. Margarita Tartakovsky, "What It Really Means to Practice Radical Acceptance," Psych Central, October 4, 2015, https://psychcentral.com/blog/what-it-really-means-to-practice-radical-acceptance#1.
3. "In Acceptance Lieth Peace" in Amy Carmichael, *Toward Jerusalem: Poems of Faith* (London: Triangle, 1987), 41.

WEEK THIRTY-NINE
1. Wayne W. LaMorte, "Behavioral Change Models: The Transtheoretical Model (Stages of Change)," Boston University School of Public Health, September 9, 2019, https://sphweb.bumc.bu.edu/otlt/mph-modules/sb/behavioralchangetheories/behavioralchangetheories6.html.
2. Liz Carter, "Why the Seasons Are Important in Our Lives," Dr Liz Carter, accessed December 8, 2021, https://www.drlizcarter.com/why-the-seasons-are-important-in-our-lives/.
3. Richard Rohr, *Jesus' Plan for a New World: The Sermon on the Mount* (Cincinnati, OH: St. Anthony Messenger Press, 1996), 37.
4. Marika Lindholm, "Combatting the Loneliness of Transition," *Psychology Today*, September 26, 2017, https://www.psychologytoday.com/us/blog/more-women-s-work/201709/combatting-the-loneliness-transition; also see Kira Asatryan, "Loneliness Has an Antidote You May Not Have Thought Of," *Psychology Today*, February 10, 2016, https://www.psychologytoday.com/us/blog/the-art-closeness/201602/loneliness-has-antidote-you-may-not-have-thought.
5. William Carlos Williams (1883–1963), "The Botticellian Trees," *Poetry*, February 1931, 267.

WEEK FORTY
1. Kyle Benson, "The Anger Iceberg," The Gottman Institute, November 8, 2016, https://www.gottman.com/blog/the-anger-iceberg/.
2. C. S. Lewis, *Surprised by Joy: The Shape of My Early Life* (New York: Harcourt Brace, 1955), 74.
3. Kendra Cherry, "Unconditional Positive Regard in Psychology," Verywell Mind, May 10, 2020, https://www.verywellmind.com/what-is-unconditional-positive-regard-2796005.

WEEK FORTY-ONE
1. Viktor E. Frankl, Goodreads, accessed November 26, 2021, https://www.goodreads.com/quotes/8144491-between-stimulus-and-response-there-is-a-space-in-that.
2. "How to Stretch Correctly and Improve Your Overall Flexibility," Realbuzz, accessed November 26, 2021, https://www.realbuzz.com/articles-interests/fitness/article/how-to-stretch-correctly-and-improve-your-overall-flexibility/.

WEEK FORTY-TWO
1. Shirley Davis, "Reparenting to Heal the Wounded Inner Child," CPTSDfoundation.org, July 27, 2020, https://cptsdfoundation.org/2020/07/27/reparenting-to-heal-the-wounded-inner-child/.
2. Davis, "Reparenting to Heal."
3. Chip Dodd, *The Voice of the Heart: A Call to Full Living* (Franklin, TN: Sage Hill, LLC, 2015), 157.

WEEK FORTY-THREE
1. Richard Rohr, "Waiting and Unknowing," Center for Action and Contemplation, December 1, 2019, https://cac.org/waiting-and-unknowing-2019-12-01/.

WEEK FORTY-FOUR
1. Oswald Chambers, "Don't Calculate without God," *My Utmost for His Highest*, July 5, accessed December 1, 2021, https://utmost.org/classic/don%E2%80%99t-calculate-without-god-classic/.
2. Morgan Harper Nichols, Tumblr, accessed December 9, 2021, https://morganharpernichols.tumblr.com/post/178500854648/you-are-not-weak-for-needing-to-rest-you-are-not.

WEEK FORTY-FIVE
1. Stephanie Hairston, "How Grief Shows Up in Your Body," WebMD, July 11, 2019, https://www.webmd.com/special-reports/grief-stages/20190711/how-grief-affects-your-body-and-mind.

2. "Takotsubo Cardiomyopathy (Broken-Heart Syndrome)," Harvard Health Publishing, January 29, 2020, https://www.health.harvard.edu/heart-health/takotsubo-cardiomyopathy-broken-heart-syndrome.

3. C. S. Lewis, *The Problem of Pain* (New York: MacMillan, 1947), 81.

WEEK FORTY-SIX

1. Zach Brittle, "Manage Conflict: Accepting Influence," The Gottman Institute, April 29, 2015, https://www.gottman.com/blog/manage-conflict-accepting-influence/.

2. L. B. Cowman, "Streams in the Desert—March 24," Crosswalk.com, March 24, 2021, https://www.crosswalk.com/devotionals/desert/streams-in-the-desert-march-24th.html.

WEEK FORTY-SEVEN

1. "The Importance of Pretend Play," *Scholastic*, accessed December 1, 2021, https://www.scholastic.com/parents/kids-activities-and-printables/activities-for-kids/arts-and-craft-ideas/importance-pretend-play.html.

WEEK FORTY-EIGHT

1. Lexico, s.v. "acceptance," accessed January 9, 2021, ACCEPTANCE English Definition and Meaning | Lexico.com

2. "The Serenity Prayer and Twelve Step Recovery," Hazelden Betty Ford Foundation, October 15, 2018, The Serenity Prayer and Twelve Step Recovery | Hazelden Betty Ford.

3. Jon Kabat-Zinn, *Coming to Our Senses: Healing Ourselves and the World through Mindfulness* (New York: Hyperion, 2005), 407.

4. Jodi Clarke, *The Five Stages of Grief*, Verywell Mind, February 12, 2021, https://www.verywellmind.com/five-stages-of-grief-4175361.

WEEK FORTY-NINE

1. Saul McLeod, "Cognitive Dissonance," Simply Psychology, February 5, 2018, https://www.simplypsychology.org/cognitive-dissonance.html.

2. John Ruskin, in L. B. Cowman, *Streams in the Desert* (Los Angeles: Oriental Missionary Society, 1925), January 22.

WEEK FIFTY-ONE

1. C. S. Lewis, *Yours, Jack: Spiritual Direction from C. S. Lewis*, ed. Paul F. Ford (New York: HarperOne, 2008), 369.

WEEK FIFTY-TWO

1. June Culp Zeitner, quoted at "What Is Lapidary," Lizzadro Museum of Lapidary Art, accessed December 9, 2021, https://lizzadromuseum.org/lapidary/#:~:text=%E2%80%9C%20What%20a%20true%20lapidary%20artist%20needs%20is,medium%20of%20their%20art.%20%E2%80%9F%20June%20Culp%20Zeitner.